KEYWORD
MASTERY

Keyword Research &
Article Marketing For Beginners

ANDREW D. MASON

Advance Praise for *Keyword Mastery: Keyword Research & Article Marketing For Beginners*

Andy, you have produced a superb book and resource on the ins and outs of keyword research, but importantly, how you use keyword research in your business; whether that's a pure online business or a bricks and mortar business.

The book is jam packed with practicable and usable information and I highly recommend it for novices and experts alike. I like to think I know my way around keyword research and I still found myself making notes as I read through it.

I recommend page 10 where you discuss the importance of understanding what 'buyer' keywords are; plus page 27 where you explain a topic that most people forget about when researching keywords...understanding this can save and make you a lot of money in your marketing.

And finally, having invested a lot in resources on keywords over the years yours does a superb job of explaining what can be complicated components of keyword research into easy to understand and follow instructions.

Well done and it gets my recommendation every time.

Neil Stafford

www.internetmarketingreview.com

A superb resource! Andy Mason has truly captured the broad scope of keyword research in this impressive work. Further to this, his passion for this area of expertise shines through in his extraordinary attention to detail, cross-categorisation of essential topics and concise expression of information within surprisingly easy to understand, step-by-step examples with which the reader can engage. All in all, a remarkable book, worth every penny!

Dale VMF

www.virtualmissfriday.co.uk

Andrew,

This book of yours provides fascinating reading of a highly specialised topic – well written and easy to understand. Not only does it give insightful and practical tips, it also offers valid guidelines and structure to relevant website content and architecture to get the competitive edge.

Keywords should form an integral element to all ongoing SEO activities allowing anyone with an ecommerce presence to make more money.

Well done!

John Harrison

www.streetwisepublications.co.uk

So, you are going to sell your 'stuff 'on the Internet! Well, be warned the biggest mistake people make is to simply hope, and not carry out the research. In my own particular field of e-book publishing, I know that metrics are the reason that writers rely on publishers to sell the books. Making your product a commercial proposition relies on a number of important factors, one of which is to understand exactly for what your target market is actually searching.

Andy Mason's book does this superbly. I like his approach – he has applied his scientific background to produce a clear, clinical and analytical master guidebook to an area that can dictate anything from website architecture, pre-product market viability to promotional copy. It's easy to follow and the essentials can be applied quickly and effectively.

Phil Gosling

www.successful-self-publishing.com

Hi Andy,

I just wanted to write to say that I am hugely impressed with the detailed approach that your book brings to keyword data and how it can be used to improve businesses. I love the suggestions on finding keywords for local businesses - it's really inspired.

Thanks again.

John Hillage

Copyright Notice

About the Author

Andrew Mason is a director of Mowbray Publishing Ltd and the founder of Keyword Research Services, which helps small and large business owners, internet marketers and ecommerce sites to significantly increase their visibility and rankings in Google. He has many years of experience in producing various publications, notably ebooks, and managing a team of specialists in order to get products to the highest possible standard.

Andrew works with his clients on a one-to-one basis and thoroughly enjoys the challenge and satisfaction of ensuring that each website that he is tasked to improve will get dedicated and personalised service in order to make more profit.

Born, bred and educated in Yorkshire in England, Andrew holds a degree in Astrophysics from the University of York and brings mathematical, diagnostic and clinical skills to the world of information publishing and ongoing internet search engine optimisation.

When he's not analysing search results and increasing his clients' web presence, he loves to indulge his long-time passion for astronomy by scanning the night sky through his 72mm refractor and 8" Schmidt-Cassegrain telescopes. He also enjoys creating digital artworks and walking his pet Labrador Phoebe.

To contact Andrew, you can reach him at:

Website: http://keywordresearchservice.co.uk

Email: info@keywordresearchservice.co.uk

Phone: +44 (0)845 031 8215

Twitter: @ADMason

Mowbray Publishing Ltd
Clifford House
7–9 Clifford Street
York YO1 9RA
England

Dedication

I would like to acknowledge and thank several people important to me who have encouraged and supported me in my life and work, not just in the creation of this book. So firstly, I'd like to thank my wife, Michelle, for her love and infinite patience and understanding while I spent evenings and weekends writing and drinking every caffeinated drink I could put my hands on. My Labrador, Phoebe, wasn't quite so understanding.

Staying in the area of family, I would also like to thank my mother and father for their limitless support and spirit of entrepreneurialism. It's a cliché, but without them this book simply wouldn't have been possible.

Table of Contents

Foreword

Before the advent of the internet, assessing the potential market for a proposed new product or service often meant expensive market research way beyond the reach of the average small business. And even then, its accuracy was questionable.

As a result, many businesses based their hopes and dreams (and no small amount of investment of both time and money) on hearsay, judgement – sound or otherwise – experience and a healthy dose of gut instinct. Some struck lucky, and their experience in, and judgement of, a market proved sound. But others found their gut instinct was not quite as reliable as they had presumed, and their foray into unchartered waters proved to be a hugely expensive mistake.

The tragedy is that small businesses are still basing proposed new products and services on the same weak and unreliable foundations, without realising that accurate and scientific market research, whether local, national or global, is but a few strokes of the keyboard away on their nearest computer. What's more, other than a relatively minimal investment of time, this research costs next to nothing to do.

Keyword research is the analysis of the words and phrases that your customers enter into search engines such as Google.

The difference after some keyword research is a product or service that has a much higher chance of success, simply because you know the potential demand before you even start, and you know the potential competition that awaits. You are therefore able to make a sound judgement on whether to invest your energy, time and money before you even start.

What's more, keyword research can lead to the discovery of new and often highly profitable markets you didn't previously realise even existed.

Mastering the skill of keyword research and using it effectively can make the difference between a highly successful product or service that creates wealth, jobs and prosperity, and one that barely makes a blip and disappears without a trace, often at considerable cost to those behind it.

As an example of what keyword research can lead to, I have personal acquaintances who, on the back of a few minutes of effective keyword research and using the same information available to you in this book, have quickly created simple businesses (often consisting of just a website with a few pages) and sold them well in excess of six figures. And they continue to repeat the process, over and over, simply because it *works*.

Others still, with keywords representing high-value acquisitions like medical equipment, vehicles, industrial machinery and consultancy, have developed businesses bringing in several million pounds a year.

So do you think keyword research might be worth your while too?

Keyword research is often mentioned in marketing circles but then quickly skirted over as a *nice to have* without any real understanding of the critical and central role it plays in much of successful marketing, online or otherwise.

As founder of SubmitYourArticle.com, I am always encouraging, if not cajoling, clients to treat keyword research as the absolutely basic and foundational step they must complete before expanding their efforts and investing further in online marketing.

Without the right foundations in place, you're simply shooting into the dark – hoping for success, but without any real knowledge, let alone certainty, that the direction in which you're heading is going to bear fruit.

Unfortunately, hope – often based on personal passions, interests and inclinations, or perhaps the *advice* of a friend or associate who thinks a business direction *might be a good way to go* but without anything solid to back up their opinion – is a very poor predictor of success. Fortunately, as you'll discover, it's incredibly easy to avoid the situation where you're hanging on the precipice and only have blind hope left to fall back on.

Andy Mason is one of the foremost experts on keyword research I know. And although I've been working online for over a decade at the time of writing and have based a lot of my own projects and online marketing activities on keyword research, I learned a lot of new information in this book that I wish I'd been aware of years ago.

You, as reader of this book, are in a very fortunate position for two reasons.

Firstly, you're lucky enough to have come across this book now, and not in five years' time. Even so, you'll still likely wish you'd had this information five years ago.

Secondly, you're smart and wise enough to be actually reading this book. My strongest recommendation, however, would be not just to read it. Study it, practise it and make the mastery of effective keyword research central to your business.

For those acquaintances of mine who have created six- and seven-figure businesses off the back of keyword research, knowledge is *everything*. You have the same knowledge in your hands right now. Read and absorb. Then read again and create effective action.

Steve Shaw

Founder, SubmitYourArticle.com

Introduction

As anyone who has owned a computer knows, there's never a good time to buy one, because the next shiny piece of hardware makes yours outdated after six months, even though it's still reliable and gets the job done. To some degree, this also applies with the internet and how information is accessed. Between emerging markets and technologies, continuous improvement processes, various marketing tools, devices and web browsers coming and going, and search engines' continuous developments to their own interfaces and algorithms, the internet isn't the unmoving *terra firma* we wish it to be. In short, at the time of printing, I have endeavoured to make everything factually correct, but as things change, so too will the accuracy of this book. The principles underpinning the practical side, however, should endure for some time to come, despite cosmetic changes to the tools discussed. Therefore, fear not if, for example, the Google AdWords Keyword Tool looks different to the way it did yesterday: at its core, the key functionality should remain.

Next, it's worth pointing out that although much can be done for free, so much more business-critical information can be extracted and applied with some well-chosen paid services. It's not that these services do anything you can't – it's merely that the processes you would have to do manually can be automated, which has *massive* time-saving implications. Some tools can work through the night on your behalf, giving you fresh data after a good night's sleep – some do your bidding for *months*, hands-free. If you value your time anywhere near as much as I do then there are two specific services that help you immensely – one for keyword research, and one for the subsequent article marketing. Both are mentioned later in the book. These tools give you *time* – time that you can use either to focus on your core business, or to improve your work–life balance.

My final point about tools is with regard to your computer's operating system and office software. Macs and Linux machines are very powerful and secure, but in the interests of the compatibility and consistency of the tools mentioned in this book, I recommend using Microsoft Windows (particularly Windows 7), because this is the platform that most business tools are written for. I also recommend using Microsoft Excel 2007 or Excel 2010 for your spreadsheets later on. It's possible to use Excel 2003 or OpenOffice Calc (a free alternative to Excel), but realistically it will make life harder because they lack the features we will use.

You may have heard the phrase 'keyword research' thrown around several times and may not know where to begin. It may be perceived to be a necessary but difficult and arcane process, more art than science. In *Chapter 1: What Is Keyword Research?* I begin to demystify and define exactly what keyword research is. Then *Chapter 2: Benefits of Keyword Research* offers clear and profound reasons as to why it's such a powerful, underrated business tool, and how it can be your secret weapon that leaves your competition several steps behind.

In *Chapter 3: The Process of Keyword Research*, I look at how to perform the illuminating process of keyword research. *Chapter 4: Advanced Techniques and Sources of Keywords* continues with alternative methods of capturing additional data for those with a healthy appetite for keywords.

In *Chapter 5: Local and Mobile Search*, I look at the exploration of keywords for local businesses, and for those businesses that actively seek strong online visibility in the exponentially proliferating market of mobile devices.

All the previous chapters and research come together in *Chapter 6: Applications of Keyword Research*, when I help you take all-important action based on the fruits of your keyword discoveries.

There are a considerable number of ways of applying what you've learnt from the research, and by far one of the most beneficial in generating leads and conversions (whether sales or enquiries) to your business is through article marketing, which I define in *Chapter 7: What Is Article Marketing?*. Then in *Chapter 8: Benefits of Article Marketing* I look at the numerous key advantages that a sustained article marketing campaign can offer.

In *Chapter 9: Caveats of Article Marketing*, I take a moment to discuss some of the practicalities to be aware of when launching a campaign.

I wrap things up by looking in depth at the 'how to' of article marketing in *Chapter 10: The Process of Article Marketing*. Make no mistake: it's not an exaggeration to say that with sufficient keyword research, implemented through a consistent, targeted article marketing campaign, your site's improved ranking in the search engines will boost subsequent conversions and return on investment (ROI) to another level.

Lastly, thank you for purchasing this book. I enjoyed writing it, and may it serve you and your business well for years to come.

Part 1

Keyword Research

1 What Is Keyword Research?

Not nearly as difficult as it is perceived to be, that's for sure.

I've lost track of the number of business owners and entrepreneurs I have spoken to who have heard 'keyword research' mentioned casually in an internet marketing book, forum or video, and heard that it's an important exercise, only to be left with a vague worry this is another process they *should* be doing, but don't know how.

The ironic thing is that the astute internet marketers are right about it being important – I can't think of another single method of gathering such a rich, practical seam of information for your business that can be used in a multitude of ways. By looking at the exact search terms your prospects use in the search engines such as Google, you gain a tremendous amount of data and insight into their wants and intentions. Allow me to convince you of the benefits of this in the next section.

One point briefly worth clarifying from the start is that a keyword can actually consist of one, two, three or more words. Therefore, despite containing three words, 'keyword research information' is actually a single keyword.

Another consideration I would like to touch on is the fact that keyword research isn't the same as search engine optimisation (SEO). They're most definitely connected, and you couldn't do one successfully without doing the other. But being an expert in one area doesn't automatically qualify you as being an expert in the other. Time for some honesty on my part: I live and breathe keyword research, and think it's the best thing since the invention of the wheel (or Google Wonder Wheel?), and if I'm ever as'
SEO advice I give the person in question a few basics. But ultimately, I ref
expert in that particular field. Likewise, I know enough about pay p
marketing, social media and public domain content to be inform

aren't my specialities. (For a list of professionals, many of which I have personally used and can recommend for these services, please see the Appendix.)

In my experience, website owners assume that their website developers have gone into the necessary depth of keyword research. If the developer explicitly mentions SEO, then the chances improve, but there is still no guarantee they have done the necessary digging. Now, I'm not suggesting that website developers don't do a thorough job – but the job of building a website has many, many elements, and there are only 24 hours in a day. It's not uncommon for keyword research to be completely new to senior marketing managers at multi-million-pound companies. So on the back of this, I offer three suggestions for what to do after reading the book:

1. Stress the importance of thorough keyword research to your web developer, and ensure they know how to do it well. You want to leave that discussion feeling confident.
2. Do it yourself. Don't panic – a little research can go a long way.
3. Ask for professional help from a keyword research specialist.

In any event, what we ultimately want to do is create an organised spreadsheet that gives us data on keyword search volumes (i.e. how many times that keyword is actually for), competition levels (based on the number and relative importance of competing sites) and commercial intent of people using those terms. This report, after being filtered for relevance, will tell us which keywords to target, and as importantly, which to disregard.

Lastly, as you progress throughout the book, you may rightly ask why I perpetually put emphasis on researching and optimising for Google. Why do Bing and Yahoo! only receive negligible attention? This is purely an objective acknowledgement of Google's share of the search engine market, and why I stress that they're the ones to rank for, what with (at the time of writing) a commanding 90%+ market share.[1] That percentage generally holds for most countries worldwide, except for the major exception of China where Baidu is the *de facto* market leader.

---

[1] Up-to-date statistics on search engine market share are available here: http://gs.statcounter.com.

The next section, *Benefits of Keyword Research*, begins to explore precisely why keyword research is such a powerful process. To jump straight into the practical details of keyword research immediately, please proceed to page 19.

2 Benefits of Keyword Research

At the start of any project, time should be set aside for dedicated keyword research. If you're midway through a project, it's still not too late for some constructive keyword research. And even for products you previously thought had reached end-of-life, it's possible to re-launch them using newly discovered keywords.

From a single, well-researched keyword report, you successfully accomplish the following points, all of which have critical business implications:

1. Removing incorrect assumptions about how people search for your product or service.
2. Pull quantitative data for your market research.
3. Judge whether you can successfully rank highly in the search engines for a particular keyword.
4. Create a list of topics to cover in your article marketing.
5. Identify your ideal internet domain names.
6. Pull pay per click (PPC) data, if you wish to run a PPC campaign.
7. Target keywords with a greater potential to convert.
8. Drive more traffic to your site.
9. Create great product names based on what people are searching for.
10. Rebrand and remonetise discontinued products.

Remove the Guesswork

It's perhaps quite hard to admit sometimes that we're closer to some projects than professional objectivity allows. Consequently (a dangerous habit), we tend to make *assumptions* about what search terms people use based on our own experiences. This means, for example, that we may be very tempted to put a lot of work into optimising our sites around industry terms or regional colloquialisms, only to later discover that they're actually useless.

Doing the research removes this counterproductive tendency, and enables you to make decisions based on data. If you're looking at a particular keyword and the numbers effectively say 'don't bother'; then don't bother. Simultaneously, some keywords that were previously (and subjectively!) dismissed as being unusable may well be worth pursuing, following analysis. Always remember that you're not your own customer.

Keyword research can and should be a critical phase of product creation, as well as part of your overall marketing toolbox. Ultimately, it allows you to use what people *actually* search for; not what you *think* they search for.

Market Research

Is the demand acceptable and encouraging? Is the competition manageable? These two questions are the foundation of market research, and both can be answered readily by looking at the search terms that are fed into, and extracted from, Google.

If you're a niche marketer, keyword research is a reliable way of judging the viability of a market you're considering. Consider these three scenarios:

1. Marketer A decides he wants to write an ebook on subject A, without doing any keyword research. He writes the book, has it formatted (either by himself or a graphic designer), maybe has a few physical copies printed, registers a domain, builds a beautiful website, pays a copywriter to write a sales letter, sets up an autoresponder sequence and contacts prospective joint venture partners. Only at this point, several months and quite a few pennies later, does he discover that there is little to no demand for the subject. And that's an expensive lesson.

2. Marketer B decides he wants to write an ebook on subject B, again without doing any keyword research, and goes through the same process. This time he *knows* there's a market. Maybe it's a popular subject on Amazon. Only now he realises that it is *far* too competitive, and even after spending hundreds of pounds per month on search engine optimisation, he can't get anywhere near the first page of Google.[2]

3. Marketer C decides he'd like to write a book on subject C, but first he does some provisional keyword research. After doing an hour's work, and possibly allowing his computer to do a few hours more work, he determines the demand and competition, and ultimately whether it will be a profitable project.

Time is our most valuable commodity. Like you, I would much rather use an hour intelligently than waste months unprofitably.

Keyword Ranking

This is related closely to the first point about removing the guesswork, but slightly more specific. As discussed in the footnote, ideally you need to be ranking for your chosen keyword in the first page of the search engine results pages (SERPs). Your ability to objectively judge whether you're more likely to rank highly for that keyword in the SERPs than the competition will be important. At first glance, you may like the look of a certain keyword, but it will be a pointless exercise chasing it if it's too competitive.

---

[2] You may ask what is so important about obtaining a position on the first page of Google. It's a fair question. How many people actually progress onto the second page, the third page etc.? Ten per cent? You'll find that figure is thrown around a lot with little in the way of citable proof to back it up. When looked at analytically, it's surprisingly difficult to get accurate statistics, although Branko Rihtman has had a serious go here: http://www.seo-scientist.com/google-ranking-ctr-click-distribution-over-serps.html. In short, if it's traffic you need, you really do need to get on page one.

Article Marketing Ideas

Article marketing is a *highly* effective method for putting your keyword research into practical use. As with keyword research, there are many reasons why article marketing should very much be included in your marketing mix. I will go into these reasons in *Chapter 8: Benefits of Article Marketing*, but for now, know that your list of keywords provides a long, specific list of possible article subjects, with numbers to back up the confidence you should have in each subject.

Article subjects are easier to come up with on some days than on others, especially if you're writing about a very specific niche. Your keyword list, by its very nature, automatically gives you hundreds of potential topics to write about.

Domain Name Ideas

If you're serious about focussing your efforts around a well-chosen keyword, particularly if you're in the early days of a project, then you need to consider buying a .com domain for that exact keyword, if it's available. This isn't critical if you have an existing website, as it's the content (and more specifically the *value* of that content) that's of paramount importance, but if you're starting from scratch, this is worth bearing in mind. Additionally, the age of your website counts in your favour – as a rule, Google prefers well-established sites to new ones.

The subject of whether or not hyphens in a domain are a good idea is a long and fiery one. My recommendation is that you stick to domains *without* hyphens, because they create more problems than they solve. It was perhaps the case in Google's infancy that it helped if the words in the domain were hyphenated for Google to be able to parse or separate and understand them. But their algorithms have improved significantly since then, and there's now no advantage to your SEO if you include hyphens. Some may argue it's easier to read domains with hyphens: compare www.thisisanexample.com to www.this-is-an-example.com. I agree, but why not remove the hyphens, make it shorter and use medial capitals (otherwise known as 'CamelCase') to differentiate words in the domain when putting it in marketing materials; for example www.ThisIsAnExample.com? Domains aren't case sensitive, so this way you have the best of both worlds.

Another reason to go for a domain *sans* hyphens: imagine repeating www.this-is-an-example.com to someone in person, over the phone, or over a radio advertisement. It will take twice as long: "Is the word 'hyphen' part of the domain? Or an actual hyphen? Do you mean hyphen or underscore?" By the time you've finished, the other person has forgotten how you started and you've probably managed to leave them none the wiser, or lost their interest altogether.

One final thing on the subject of domain registration. You may well find that your exact match domain has gone. If you feel that the keyword (e.g. 'This Is An Example') is *still* worth including in the domain and you'd objectively really rather not consider alternatives then try adding a stop word at the beginning or end, e.g. review, info, online. In terms of search engine optimisation, this *keyword rich domain* (that contains your keyword and a stop word, such as www.ThisIsAnExampleInfo.com or www.ThisIsAnExampleOnline.com) is almost (though not quite) as good as having the full, *exact match domain* (that contains your keyword only: www.ThisIsAnExample.com).

Pay Per Click Data

In the same keyword report that we learn how to create in Chapter 3, it's really no extra work to pull pay-per-click (PPC) information on each and every keyword.

On the Google results page, the PPC advertisements are those to the right and sometimes above the organic search results. The PPC ads are capable of 'jumping the queue' and featuring on the first page of Google – however, it costs the advertiser every time they're clicked, and you'll probably pay more to get it right to the top of the pile.

PPC, or AdWord, campaigns can be both long- and short-term: if you've spent a while testing and improving your site and are confident of your conversion rates, it makes absolute sense to put money into this, since from experience you *know* what your ROI will be. Similarly, you may wish to intensively test a new sales letter or squeeze page (i.e. a page with an opt-in form and no outbound links, created primarily for list-building purposes). In which case, a mini-PPC campaign doesn't take long to set up, starts gathering data quickly (assuming your keywords and ads are approved), and lets you run the test to tightly controlled timescales and budgets.

PPC information lets you gauge how affordable a process setting up some AdWord ads will be. If you initially looked at a competitive keyword that costs a minimum of $10 per click to be seen on the first page, this may eat up your daily budget pretty fast, and you may want to scan through your master keyword list for several cheaper, promising alternatives.

Best practices for PPC campaigns are beyond the scope of this book, but a truly excellent introduction by Perry Marshall – 'The Definitive Guide to Google AdWords' – is available here: http://www.perrymarshall.com/adwords.

High-Converting Keywords

Identifying keywords that tick the demand and competition boxes is good, but you need to really concentrate on the keywords that *convert*. You may choose to define a conversion in your own terms, whether you achieve a direct sale, a new subscriber to your mailing list or a telephone enquiry, but at the end of the day attracting real business through your site is what matters.

This is a good moment to introduce the concept of the 'buying cycle', or buying process, which is the sequence every person goes through when spending money, right from the moment they have a personal or professional interest in a subject (or have a problem) to the moment they open their wallets and pay for a product or service (and find the solution). Incidentally, your own offline advertising may well trigger the beginning of the buying cycle.

Once a need or desire has been identified and the research has begun, keywords are general and short. Someone beginning to take an interest in astronomy may use the keyword 'telescope'. This is known as *informational intent*: the beginner is trying to research very general information, such as the different types of telescope, which may be most suitable, basic capabilities, pros and cons etc.

Fig. 1: The Buying Cycle.

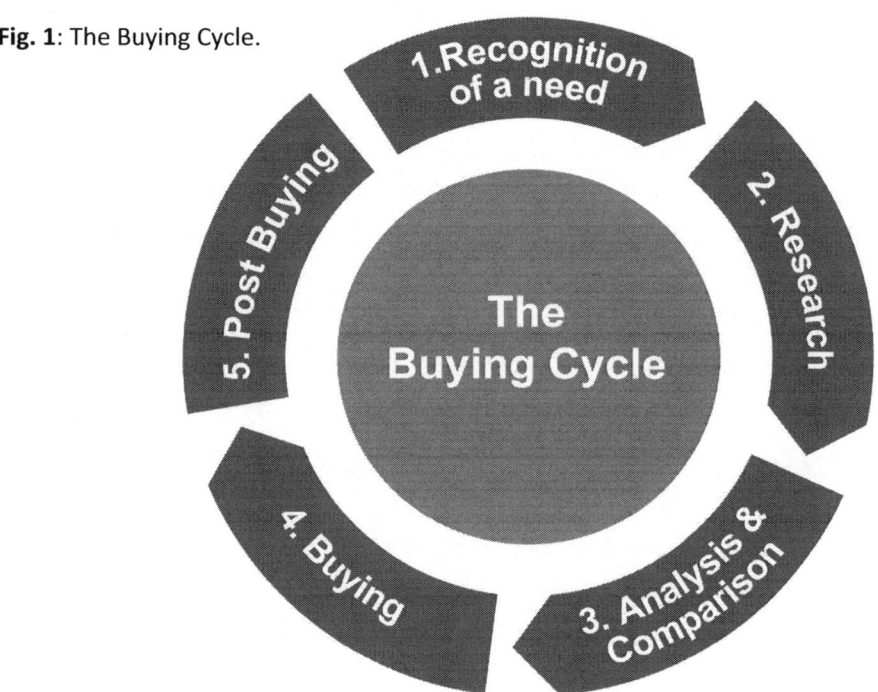

Then they start to be more specific about a make they feel comfortable with and search for 'Meade telescope'. Now they're interested in identifying a specific model, cost information, warranty information and user reviews. They progress through the buying cycle, and the search may now evolve into 'Meade LX90 Schmidt Cassegrain telescope'. All the while, the keyword is becoming longer and *more specific*.

Finally, the search is unmistakably of *transactional intent*: 'Meade LX90 Schmidt Cassegrain telescope Leeds'. It is at this stage that several telescope websites are located and studied, and risk is addressed and reduced. This is the test of the quality of your site and its ability to sell: good content, usability, client testimonials, competitive pricing, secure payment systems, copywriting and guarantees all work together to convince this person that you're trustworthy.

Once this individual settles on a single site, the order is made. If the person is happy with the delivery, the product and the follow-up service and support, they then become a *brand advocate* who is happy to promote your products for free, by word of mouth, social networking sites or other channels. This can bring you back to the beginning of the cycle, as someone else, in turn, recognises that they also have an interest in amateur astronomy and begins their own research.

It's important to identify those keywords that are more likely to convert, and the likelihood is higher for *long-tail keywords* that are searched for at the closing stages of the buying cycle. (See the final section in this chapter regarding long-tail keywords.) These are harder to find because they're more specific and the search volumes are lower, but it's absolutely worth your time as you're now targeting those in the mindset to make a purchase. If your competition isn't identifying these long-tail keywords, you can give your business a significant strategic advantage.

Note: It's not only longer keywords that can be specific; there are exceptions. 'Helioseismology Stanford' and 'Neurogastroenterology London' are only two-word keywords, but it's clear that whoever is using these exact terms already has a very clear idea about what they're searching for.

Divide and Conquer

As a rule, the more demand (i.e. monthly search volume) a keyword has, the more competition it has. Anyone interested in keywords is explicitly in the business of identifying the exceptions to this rule: finding closely related keywords with respectable search volumes, but those with lower competition that have drifted through the net. Keywords that may have been missed or dismissed by your competitors, but on which you can capitalise.

How? Imagine you have an ideal keyword with a high search volume, but you also have high competition. You *could* try to optimise your site for it, but it will be expensive and time-consuming, and that's if you get anywhere at all. But this is where you can be tactically smart. Do some exploring around that keyword and it's perfectly possible to identify ten long-tail variations. Because they are longer, *individually* they will have a lower monthly search volume, but *cumulatively* they can match or even exceed your original, ideal keyword, and be much less competitive in the process.

To summarise: you can target and successfully rank for several easier keywords with a high cumulative search volume, rather than a single, impossibly competitive keyword.[3]

Product Name Ideas

If you're firmly in the product creation or branding phase, a name for a product may not naturally suggest itself too readily. To quote the grandmaster of advertising, David Ogilvy:

> *"I don't know the rules of grammar... If you're trying to persuade people to do something, or buy something, it seems to me you should use their language, the language they use every day, the language in which they think. We try to write in the vernacular."*

David Ogilvy, quoted in Denis Higgins, *The Art of Writing Advertising: Conversations with Masters of the Craft*

In the 21st century, this directly translates as: use your customers' *search query language*, so you can identify what your customer wants and how they search for it. As a quick example, there are 110,000 global monthly exact searches for 'backpacks'. 'Rucksacks' are exactly the same thing, but this time there are only 14,800 global

---

[3] As a side note, something very similar happens in a technology known as *grid computing*, whereby an immensely complicated problem isn't solved by a single, powerful supercomputer, but instead the problem is broken up and distributed to many thousands of far less powerful spare home computers (voluntarily, of course). One such project is Folding@home, which simulates the behaviours of protein folding in an effort to better understand diseases such as Alzheimer's and cancer, and has produced many scientific research papers. In February 2009, the *cumulative* power of these ordinary, home computers exceeded 5 petaflops, or 5 quadrillion calculations per second. By comparison, the fastest IBM supercomputer, at the time, managed only 1.105 petaflops. (One quadrillion = 1,000,000,000,000,000.)

monthly searches; less than a seventh that of 'backpacks'. As you can see, this attention to specificity will make a considerable difference to the results of your marketing strategy, both online and offline.

It's important to remember to make keywords work for you. Companies that understand their customers' search language use this data to influence every potential introduction opportunity with their target market.

Rebrand Discontinued Products

As an extension to the previous point regarding product name ideas, during new product development, what if the data was put to use rebranding products at the other end of the product lifecycle? One of your products may be experiencing a decline, but that doesn't necessarily mean it's reaching its end-of-life. If you identify a prospective keyword that you could attach to your product in the marketing, it's possible to remonetise a product you previously thought unprofitable.

Now I have discussed the benefits of identifying the right keywords, the next section begins to explore the specific benefits of searching for *longer* keywords.

Long-Tail Keywords

The graph in Fig. 2 displays the typical relationship between the search volume and the competition of keywords in a specific niche. Looking at the decreasing shape of this graph it's easier to illustrate, for several important reasons explained shortly, why long-tail keywords should be researched, identified and applied to your advertising, both online (SEO, PPC and email marketing) and offline (radio, direct mail and display ads). They're called long-tail keywords because they appear in the right hand 'tail' of the distribution.

Whilst being known to mathematicians since the 1940s, it was in a 2004 essay by *Wired* magazine's current editor-in-chief, Chris Anderson, that the long-tail concept was influentially reintroduced. In short, he saw the potential of the internet and 'the efficient economics of online retail to aggregate a large inventory of relatively low sellers'.[4] Basically, high-street stores have fundamental space limitations and can only afford to store those items that are current bestsellers. However, with an online business selling digital products, you can open up the portfolio of products and begin to sell a wider range of items with lower demand. Cumulatively, more revenue can be generated from selling a wide range of low-demand products than from a narrow range of high-demand, high-competition products.

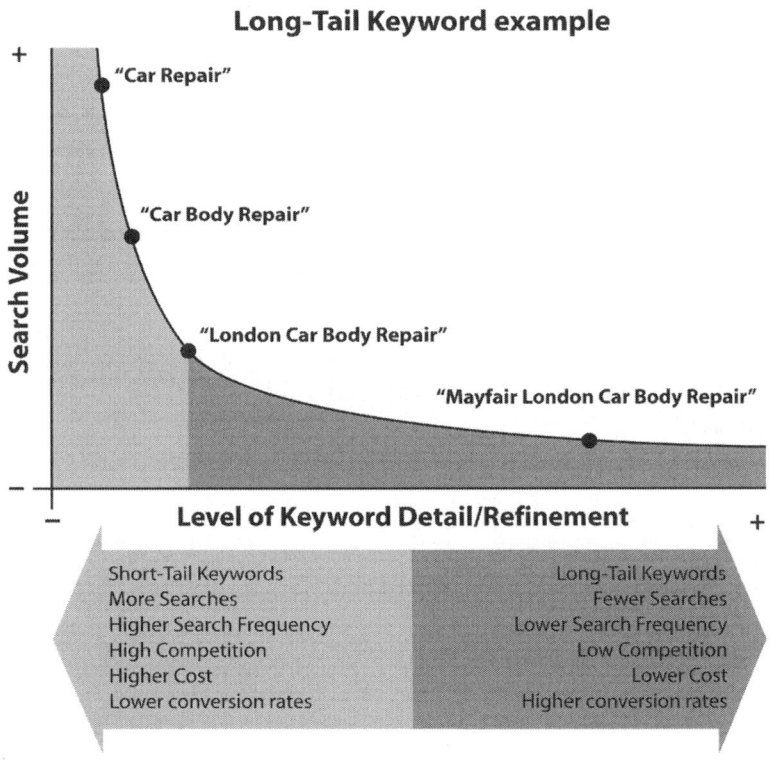

Fig. 2: Long-Tail Keywords. To the left are shorter keywords with high search volumes and high competition. To the right are the long-tail keywords with lower search volume and lower competition; however, both sides have large commercial potential.

---

[4] Chris Anderson, *The Long Tail: Why the Future of Business Is Selling Less of More*. (2006)

The same applies to keyword research. In a competitive market, many choose to throw all their business resources behind trying to optimise their site for shorter keywords, often referred to as *head terms*, *head keywords* or *root keywords*. As outlined in the previous section, these words have high search volume, which is appealing to the untrained eye. However, for several important reasons, they should be disregarded. Root keywords tend to:

1. be very highly competitive
2. be used by those with informational intent
3. take longer to rank in the SERPs
4. have low clickthrough rates and, ultimately, low conversion rates. (A clickthrough rate is a useful metric and is calculated from the number of times a link is displayed divided by the number of times it is actually clicked. For example, if a PPC advert has 200 displays [technically called *impressions*] and is clicked twice, the clickthrough rate (or CTR) is 1%.)

Conversely, long-tail keywords tend to:

1. be less competitive
2. be used by those with transactional intent
3. be ranked more quickly in the SERPs
4. have higher clickthrough rates and higher conversion rates.

Therefore, take as an example for your project Strategy A, which may involve spending time, money and energy trying to optimise for a single root keyword. This may be a tremendously difficult exercise, especially if dealing with a competitive, national (or even regional) market, and particularly if your target is to reach the top three positions on the first page of the Google results.

However, example Strategy B involves optimising your campaigns around *several* long-tail keywords, driving more targeted visitors to your site. For example, say you own a site selling backpacks. 'Backpacks' has 110,000 exact searches per month and will be up against stiff competition. Note the following slightly longer keywords and their respective monthly search volumes:

- [jansport backpacks][5] (40,500)
- [laptop backpack] (18,100)
- [kids backpacks] (12,100)
- [dakine backpacks] (12,100)
- [leather backpack] (9,900)
- [roxy backpacks] (8,100)
- [swiss gear backpack] (8,100)
- [school backpacks] (8,100)
- [hello kitty backpack] (8,100)

Cumulatively, there are 125,100 searches here, which already *exceeds* the number of searches for 'backpacks' on its own. And due to their increased specificity, these in all likelihood will lead to higher conversion rates. This is merely scratching the surface – there are many hundred unique searches for backpacks based on brand, function ('hiking backpacks', 'travel backpacks', 'dog backpack'), celebrities ('Justin Bieber backpack'), cartoon characters ('Buzz Lightyear backpack'), budget ('designer backpacks', 'cheap backpacks'), material ('ultralight backpacking', 'waterproof backpack') and accessories ('backpacking tents', 'backpacker magazine'). Furthermore, all these keywords can be segmented or grouped together to provide a framework for your website architecture, which is explained by Walter Mclean in Guest Section 2, using an SEO case study.

Do you believe this research methodology could successfully be applied to your business?

After going into some detail as to *why* you should perform keyword research, let's now look at *how*.

---

[5] These keywords are in square brackets to show these search figures use Google's *Exact* match type: I explain the critical difference between *Exact*, *Phrase* and *Broad* match types in the next chapter.

3 The Process of Keyword Research

Here's where you begin the practical process of researching and identifying the highly targeted keywords that revolve around your business.

Identify the Root Keyword

We'll start gently. Remember I mentioned root keywords previously on page 16? You need to identify the simplest, most general description of your business in as few words as possible; preferably in one or two words. Let's say I'm writing an ebook on Leonardo da Vinci, and I'm publishing and marketing it myself so I need to build my keyword list. So take 'da vinci' as the root keyword.

Create the Basic Keyword List

I'd like to introduce the most important tool you'll use within your keyword research: the Google AdWords Keyword Tool, located at:

https://adwords.google.com/select/KeywordToolExternal

You can either type this address into your browser, or just type 'keyword tool' into Google. The tool should be right at the top.

Tip: it will also be to your advantage if you sign in (using the link in the top right-hand corner) with your existing Google account details. If you don't log in, the tool will return 100 results; once logged in, the tool will serve up 800 results. If you don't have an

---

existing Google account, it's straightforward enough to get one by clicking on *Sign In* and then *Start now* and following the sign-up instructions. You will see the screen in Fig. 3

Fig. 3: The Google AdWords Keywords Tool interface.

Note: to capture and save pay per click data, it's critical that we select *Approximate CPC (Search)* under the Columns menu at the right-hand side. If this isn't selected, only global and local search volume data will be displayed.

There are a couple of tweaks we need to make before we put the root keyword 'da vinci' into the *Word or phrase* field.

Firstly, untick 'Broad' under the *Match types* setting on the left-hand side, and tick 'Exact'.

The difference is important:

With **Broad** match types, Google will return monthly search volumes for any search that remotely relates to your keyword. So searches for 'leonardo', 'da vinci paintings', 'de vinci' and 'davinci' (note the misspellings) will all be included in the totals, which is why using Broad match will yield 5,000,000 monthly searches. These figures aren't sufficiently accurate for our needs.

With **Phrase** match types, we begin to narrow down and count the number of search terms that include the keyword phrase somewhere in the user's search phrase. Therefore, 'da vinci paintings' would be included in the count, but 'leonardo', 'de vinci' and 'davinci' would *not*. As we begin to be more specific and eliminate less relevant searches, the monthly search volume should be less; and indeed it is, with 3,350,000 searches. The Phrase option is far better than Broad for your keyword research.

With **Exact** match types, we now count the number of searches for the exact keyword, with no variations or reinterpretations, prefixes or suffixes. Google searches that were 'da vinci' *only* will be counted, so even 'da vinci paintings' will not be counted this time. Again, as we become even more specific, the count will be less: 165,000 in this case. This is definitely the best option to use when researching potential domain keywords, or running a PPC campaign.

Notice the difference in numbers between Broad and Exact searches: a more than 30-fold decrease. However, Phrase or Exact are the types we must use, as it gives us the most realistic and relevant search numbers. For this exercise, I will use Exact.

The second tweak concerns the *Advanced Options and Filters* option, immediately above the Search button (shown in Fig. 4).

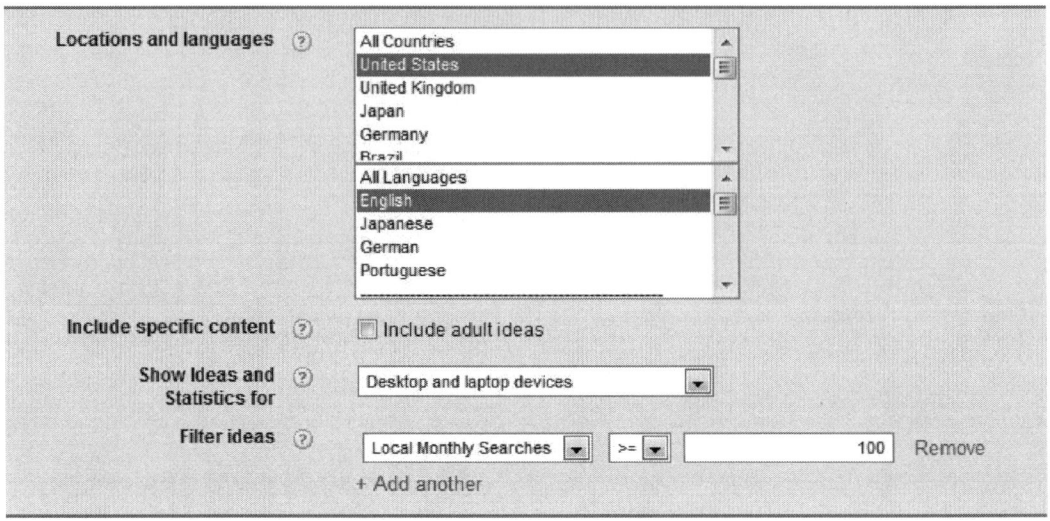

Fig. 4: The *Advanced Options and Filters* interface.

Based on the service area of your business, it's best to select your location from where Google retrieves the results. So if you're a regional or national business, select 'United Kingdom' if you're based in the UK, 'United States' if based in the US etc. If you're an international business or you're running an ecommerce site that doesn't need to limit itself to a single country, select 'All Countries'.

Lastly, it's a good idea to filter out keywords with very low monthly search volumes, and this can easily be enabled by entering '100' next to the *Local Monthly Searches* field at the bottom of this section. It's better to filter these keywords out at this stage, because the tool then reselects alternative keywords. If you wait until later to filter them out, you lose the keywords with low search volume, but they're not replaced with useful alternatives with search volumes that meet your criteria.

Now is the time to put the keyword into the *Word or phrase* field and hit *Search*. You'll probably see something very similar to the screenshot in Fig 5.

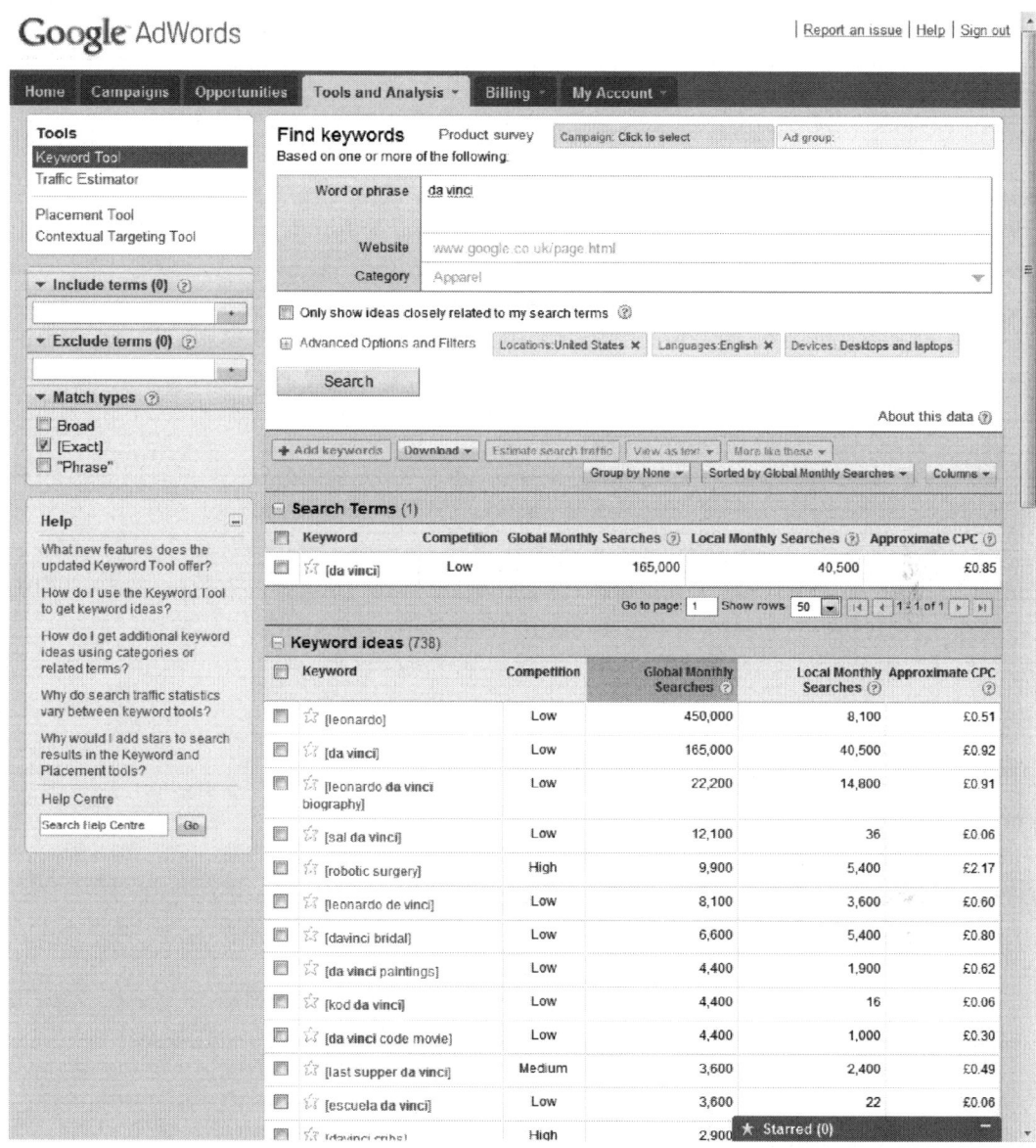

Fig. 5: The resulting keywords using 'da vinci' as the root keyword. Note: Exact match type is selected, not the default of Broad.

Note: Ensure that the *Keyword ideas* tab is selected, not *Ad group ideas*, otherwise the CSV file you save will have an extra 'Ad Group' column, which at this stage overcomplicates matters.

Notice how the keywords have been sorted by *Global Monthly Searches*, just to get an idea of the most popular search terms.

If all looks well, we'll now save them by clicking on *Download* (underneath the Search button), selecting 'All', and then selecting 'CSV'[6] next to the *Format* option. Then hit *Download*. Save it to a new, dedicated folder because we'll need to keep things organised. Leave the Google keyword tool page open because we'll be returning to it.

Summary:

1. Launch the Google AdWords Keyword Tool by typing 'keyword tool' into Google, and select the top result.
2. Enter the root keyword in the *Word or phrase* field.
3. Select the 'Exact' match type, and deselect 'Broad'.
4. Select the most relevant location information and minimum search volume (100 recommended) under the *Advanced Options and Filters* section.
5. Hit *Search*, and download the results as a CSV file into a new folder.

Expand the Keyword List

Now we'll need to look at these results and begin the process of drilling down.

Firstly, open up the CSV file. Excel 2010 does an admirable job of doing this, and it should look similar to Fig. 6

The keywords are in square brackets because we used the Exact match type. If we had used the Phrase match type, they would be in double quotation marks. If we had used the Broad match type, there would be no punctuation marks at all.

---

[6] Short for 'comma-separated values'; a type of simple data file.

If you didn't sort the list before you saved it then do so now. Click the *Sort & Filter* button in the top right-hand corner, and then *Custom Sort*. In the following box, ensure 'My data has headers' is ticked. Select to sort by 'Global Monthly Searches'; under *Order*, select 'Largest to Smallest'; and then click *OK*.

Keyword	Competition	Global Monthly Searches	Local Monthly Searches (United States)	Approximate CPC (£)
[da vinci]	0.02	165000	40500	0.85
[leonardo]	0	450000	8100	0.51
[da vinci]	0.06	165000	40500	0.92
[leonardo da vinci biography]	0.01	22200	14800	0.91
[robotic surgery]	0.69	9900	5400	2.17
[leonardo de vinci]	0.01	8100	3600	0.6
[davinci bridal]	0.23	6600	5400	0.8
[da vinci paintings]	0.13	4400	1900	0.62
[da vinci code movie]	0.06	4400	1000	0.3
[last supper da vinci]	0.46	3600	2400	0.49
[davinci cribs]	1	2900	2900	1.09
[da vinci last supper]	0.11	2900	1300	0.57
[davincis]	0	2400	2400	0.6
[da vinci inventions]	0.06	2400	1300	1.43
[da vinci bridal]	0.22	2400	1600	0.74
[da vinci surgery]	0.7	2400	1600	1.5
[leonardo da vinci s inventions]	0.05	2400	1300	0.06
[the last supper leonardo da vinci]	0.04	2400	880	0.66
[da vinci cannon]	0.06	2400	480	0.52
[da vinci surgical system]	0.49	1900	1300	0.85
[da vinci quotes]	0	1900	1000	0.06
[davinci beads]	0.92	1900	1900	0.28
[davinci syrup]	1	1600	1600	0.56
[da vinci hotel]	0.34	1600	260	0.69

Fig. 6: Reviewing initial results from the Google AdWords Keyword Tool.

Now we must build on this data by selecting related words from this list with higher search volumes, and running them *each in turn* through the Google keyword tool. Therefore, from the list, we could argue the following are the most highly-searched-for related keywords:

[leonardo]   [da vinci paintings]

[leonardo da vinci biography]   [last supper da vinci]

[da vinci last supper]	[the last supper leonardo da vinci]
[da vinci inventions]	[da vinci quotes]
[leonardo da vinci s inventions]	[leonardo vinci]

We have already searched using 'da vinci', so that has been omitted. Similarly, omit your own root keyword from this set of expanded keywords. In this case, we will now run each of these back through the Google keyword tool. Unfortunately, there are no shortcuts to this part, but it doesn't take too long with a bit of practice, and it's a key step in your keyword research. It's important that these new CSV files are also saved in the same folder as the original CSV file.

The tool will actually accept several keywords at once, by starting each new one on a new line. However, you will gain more keywords by running them through separately.

To help keep track of the keywords you have run through the tool, you should do two things:

1. Select the cell containing the keyword and change the *Fill Colour*, using the bucket icon in the *Font* section of the menu bar.
2. When saving the CSV file, rename it from something like *keyword_ideas_20120126_0651730.csv* to *your keyword*.csv, e.g. *da vinci paintings.csv*. This also prevents you from accidentally running the same keyword twice, because Windows will prompt you if you try to save the file using the same filename as an existing file.

This part becomes subjective, based primarily on your patience, as you could continue re-running more related keywords back through the keyword tool. You will discover more keywords and expand your list with each additional keyword search. You could, however, define beforehand how many additional keywords you wish to analyse, for example:

- As we have done here, we could choose a fixed number of extra keywords. So commit to analysing an extra 10, 20 or even 50 well-chosen keywords from your original 'master' list.

- Alternatively, we could choose to use keywords over a certain search volume threshold, thereby running every keyword through with over 1,000 searches per month. If you're focussing on a local or highly niche service, search volumes will naturally be lower, so use keywords accordingly, such as keywords with 500 or even 100 monthly searches.

Once complete, we now have a folder full of CSV files which we now need to merge into a single, meaningful set of keyword data.

It's worth highlighting that these Google search volume figures aren't entirely accurate, and should be used as a guide only. Due to some quite considerable rounding of the numbers by Google, we'll never know in absolute terms *precisely* how many searches are made of a certain keyword, but we can use the numbers to tell us which perform better in *relative* terms.

Negative Keywords

In the process of expanding your keyword list you'll be doing yourself a favour by beginning to identify and filter out keywords that you have no intention of using in your campaigns. These are known as *negative keywords*. For instance, words such as 'free' and 'cheap' offer insight into the prospects' mind, identifying those who probably aren't willing to spend money on their problem. You should make a note of these and include them in the Google AdWords Keyword Tool's 'Exclude terms' field. Henceforth, no keyword containing that phrase will be included in the results.

There are other groups of words called 'homonyms' and 'homographs' that may be spelt the same as some of your keywords, but whose meaning is totally different and, therefore, irrelevant. For instance, if your campaign focuses on golf, you may well find references to the Volkswagen Golf, so 'Volkswagen' and 'VW' are your negative keywords.

Finally, you will probably notice reoccurring negative keywords that you'll only be aware of once you start the research process. They may be unwanted because of the context you wish to apply them; they may be unwanted because they contain the names of towns or cities nowhere near your service area; or they may be unwanted because they contain common misspellings. In our example, notice how 'robotic surgery' has surfaced as a suggested keyword. 'da Vinci' is also the name of a robotic surgical system, so in this context, 'robot' and 'surgery' are valid negative keywords. Similarly, in order to maintain relevance, if we ran 'Leonardo' through the tool, 'DiCaprio' could be excluded from the results.

If you spot several instances of these negative keywords then they're worth excluding in the tool. However, if you're only spotting single instances then it's not worth the time taken to remove these negative keywords individually – simply ignore them later on.

This step greatly improves the relevance of your keywords, which in the end leads to higher conversions.

Merge Files

We now have to merge all the data from the CSV files into a single, new CSV file. There are standalone, paid tools you can use to do this. However, there are two ways to accomplish the same thing for free: manually, and automatically. The automatic way can be very quick indeed. Your preference will probably boil down to your experience, knowledge and confidence using the Command Prompt in Windows, but you only need to use three simple lines of code (perhaps even one), so don't be discouraged from using the automatic method.

Manually

You open each CSV file in turn, copy the contents and paste them into a master CSV file. The pro: it's easy. The con: monotony is an understatement, especially if you have more than five CSV files, which you probably will. This alone is why I recommend the automatic method.

To merge them manually, open the master keyword list (File **A**) and the first of the additional CSV files (File **B**).

1. From File **B**, click on any cell that contains data.
2. Now select all the data in File **B** by pressing *Ctrl + A*.
3. Copy this data by pressing *Ctrl + C*.
4. Open File **A**, the master file, and scroll right to the bottom, where you run out of data.
5. Select the cell immediately under the last keyword, and paste in the data by pressing *Ctrl + V*. The new data should appear.
6. Leave File **A** open, and close File **B**.

Now repeat for the remaining CSV files: copy the contents of each, and paste them at the bottom of the master keyword list. Your master list will expand as each set of keywords is added to it. You will notice many duplicated keywords, which I address in the next step.

Automatically

You have a folder full of CSV files – this method uses the Command Prompt and merges the lot in seconds. Follow the next steps and you'll soon get the hang of it.

For XP users:

You have to do a little more work than Windows 7 users, but fortunately, not too much more.

1. Place your Keywords folder directly at the root of your C: drive, so it sits alongside your Windows and Program Files folders. Copying and pasting your folder here is probably easiest[7] (see Fig. 7).

---

[7] I have included this step to standardise and simplify the location of your Keywords folder. If you're happy navigating to your Keywords folder using the *Command Prompt* directory commands, please do that and skip to Step 7.

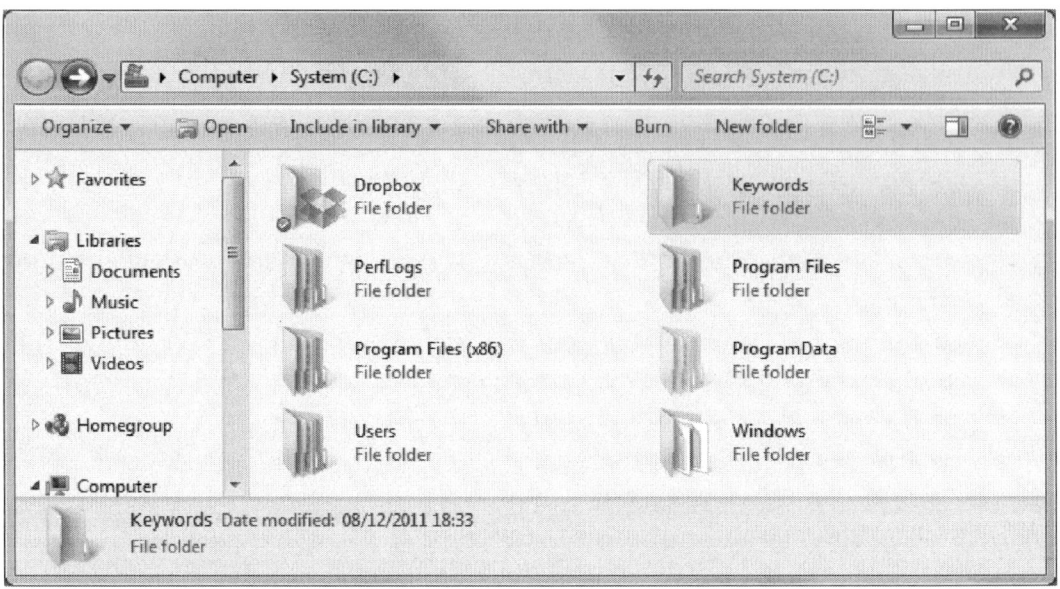

Fig. 7: Creating a new Keywords folder in the C: drive.

2. Click on the *Start* button, and from the menu, select *Run*. (Alternatively, locate the *Run* dialogue box in the *Start Menu* → *All Programs* → *Accessories* folder.)
3. Type **cmd** and click *OK* or hit the *Enter* button:

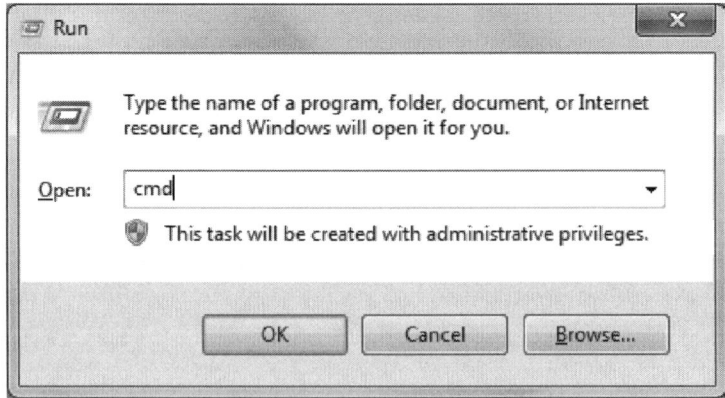

Fig. 8: The *Run* window.

4. The following *Command Prompt* should appear (except with your name).

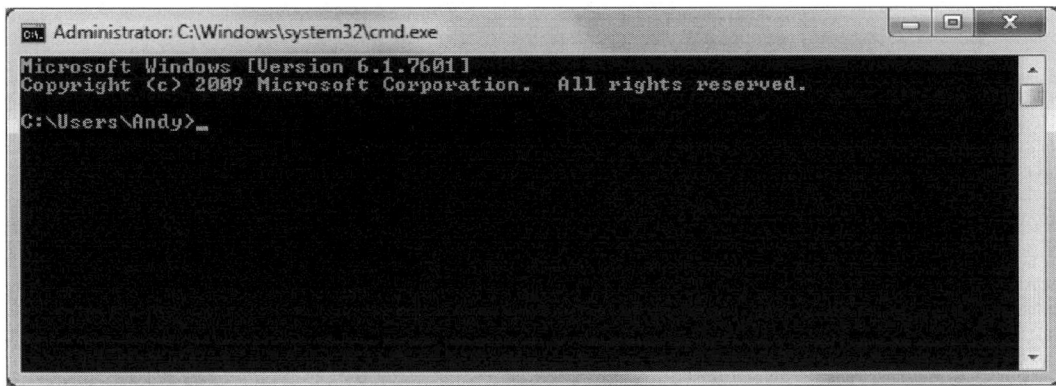

Fig. 9: The basic *Command Prompt* window.

5. Type **cd..** (including the dots) and press *Enter*. Do this step *twice*:

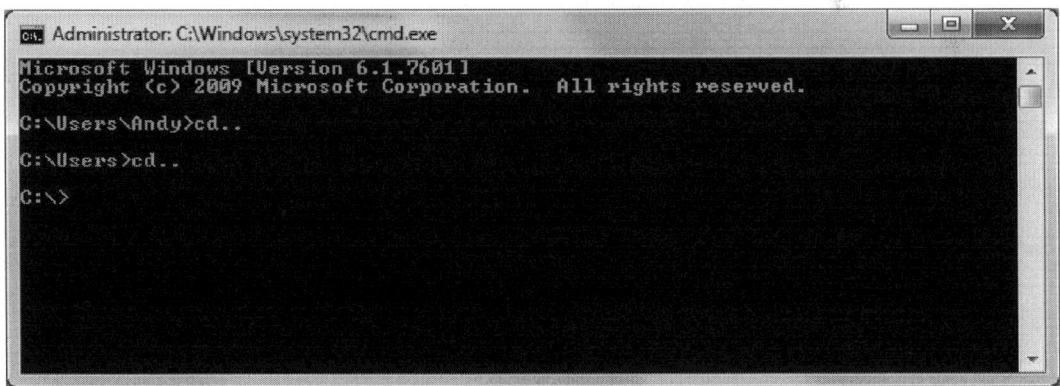

Fig. 10: The *Command Prompt*, following step 5.

6. Type **cd Keywords** (or the exact name of your Keywords folder, whatever you've elected to name it) and press *Enter*:

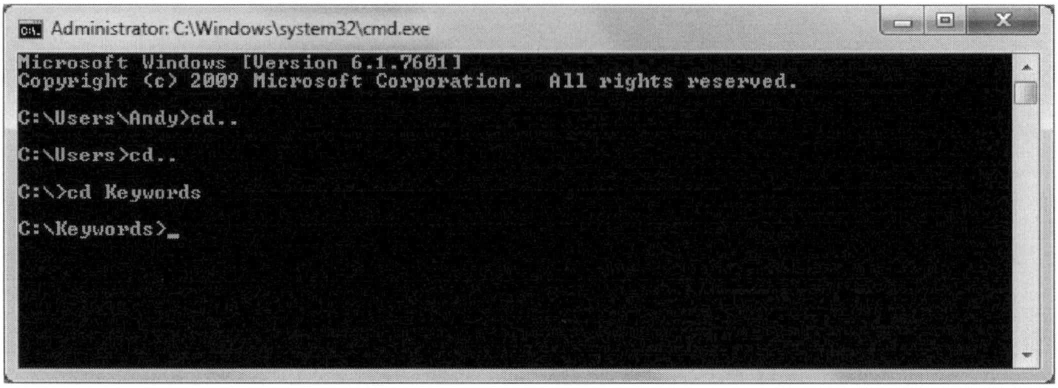

Fig. 11: The *Command Prompt*, where we are now in the correct Keywords directory.

7. Ensuring you don't have an existing file named 'all.csv', type **copy *.csv ALL.csv** and hit *Enter*:

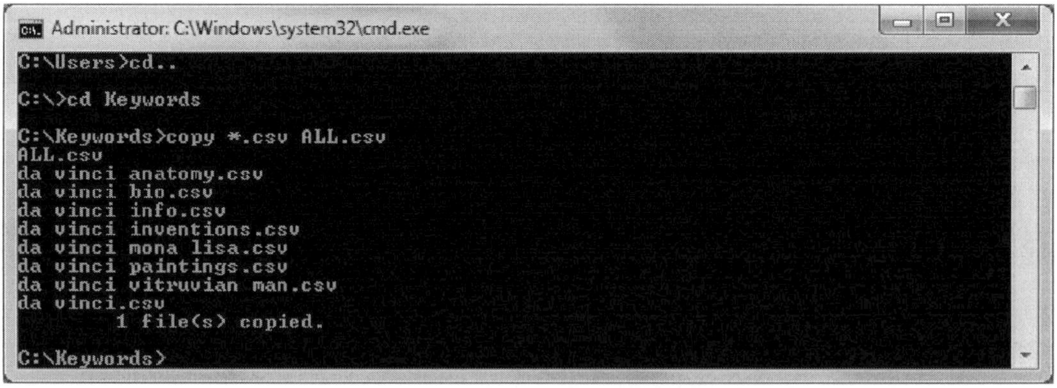

Fig. 12: The *Command Prompt*, following the easy merger of all CSV files.

8.   Type **exit** and hit *Enter* to close the *Command Prompt*. Job done. You now have a master CSV file named ALL.csv in your Keywords folder into which all of the CSV files are merged.

For Vista and Windows 7 users:

The first step here effectively performs Steps 1–6 above in one stroke. To begin, locate your Keywords folder. Normally, if you right click on a folder, the first two options in the context menu are:

Fig. 13: The top entries in the menu when right clicking on a folder.

However, when holding *Shift* and right clicking in Vista or Windows 7, two more options appear:

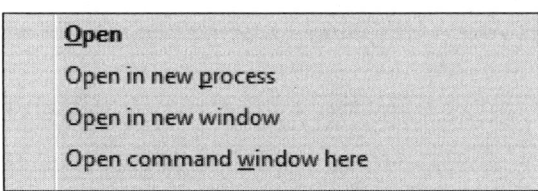

Fig. 14: The top entries in the menu when right clicking on a folder when holding *Shift*.

1. Hold *Shift* and right click on your Keywords folder (the location doesn't matter), then left click on *Open command window here*:

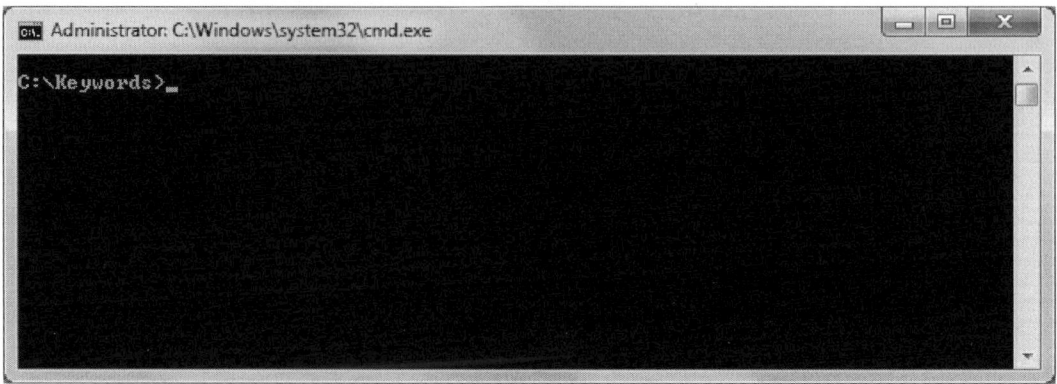

Fig. 15: The basic *Command Prompt* window.

2. As before, ensuring you don't have an existing file named 'all.csv', type **copy *.csv ALL.csv** and hit *Enter*:

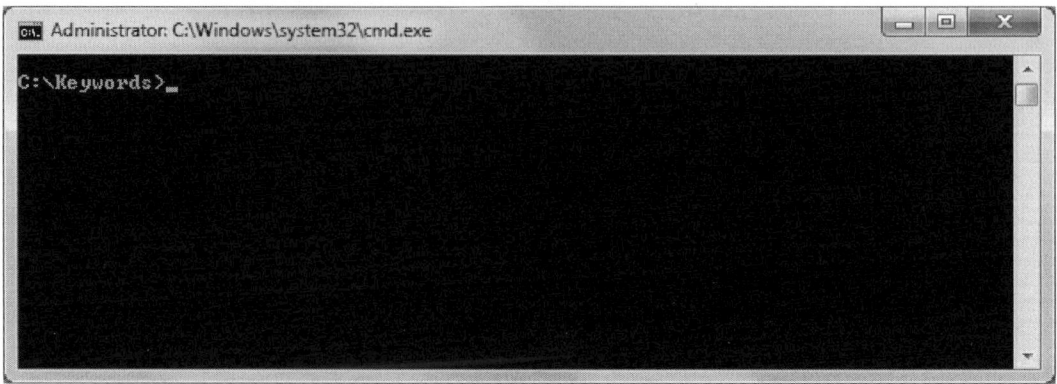

Fig. 16: The *Command Prompt*, following the easy merger of all CSV files.

3. Type **exit** and hit *Enter*. You now have a master CSV file named ALL.csv in your Keywords folder.

With practice you can merge dozens or even hundreds of CSV files in seconds, because this method only involves two mouse clicks and a single *Command Prompt* command.

Lastly, you may be concerned that you will reach Excel's row limit by the sheer volume of keywords. This only becomes a concern if you merge more than 80 files, all of which contain 800 keywords, which is unlikely. Excel 2003 can handle 65,536 (or 2^{16}) rows, and Excel 2007 and Excel 2010 can both handle 1,048,576 (or 2^{20}) rows. After the duplicate keywords are removed, we will then have a manageable level of unique keywords.

Removing Duplicates

Since we have combined several spreadsheets together, our new CSV file contains many unnecessarily duplicated keywords, which need purging.

For this step, Excel 2007 or Excel 2010 is recommended, because they perform this task quickly and easily.

1. Open your new ALL.csv file.
2. Click on any cell that contains data.
3. Go to the Data tab, and click on *Remove Duplicates*:

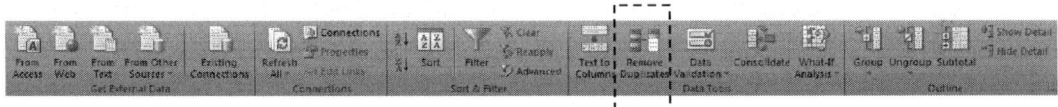

Fig. 17: The Data tab. *Remove Duplicates* is two thirds of the way along.

4. Click *Unselect All*. Ensure 'My data has headers' is ticked.
5. Put a tick next to 'Keyword' (every other column header should be unselected).
6. Click *OK*.

You will receive a notification to say how many duplicated entries there were and how many unique entries (i.e. keywords) remain. You should now save this duplicate-free keyword file.

Sort the List

Congratulations – we now have a core set of keywords we can begin to use.

I recommend spacing your columns out, so that they're less bunched up, by dragging the right-hand boundary at the top of the column. There are four new column headers we now need to create: *Length*, *Formula*, *Competing Sites* and *PageRank*:

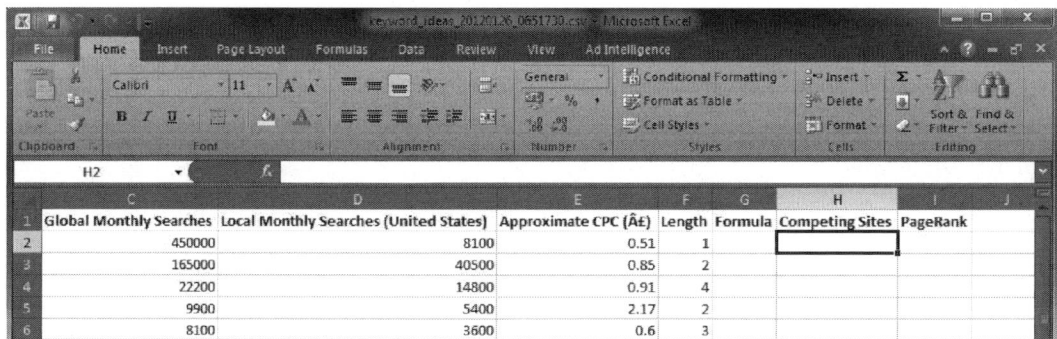

Fig. 18: The spreadsheet with the addition of the four new column headers.

Length

We're going to determine the number of words from which each keyword is composed, remembering that, in general, longer keywords are better. For example, the keyword 'leonardo da vinci biography' has a length of four.

To the right of the *Approximate CPC* column, create a new column entitled *Length*. In the cell underneath this, type the following code, including the equals sign:

=LEN(A2)-LEN(SUBSTITUTE(A2," ",""))+1

If done successfully, the cell will now contain the word count of your first keyword.

Now we must apply this code to every keyword - this is done easily. Hover the mouse pointer exactly on the bottom right-hand corner of the cell, and it will change its icon to a narrow 'plus' sign. Hold down the left mouse button and drag it down to the bottom of the spreadsheet: the code is now replicated all the way and provides a word count of every keyword.

Formula

Now sort the keywords based on both search volume and keyword length, using a simple formula.

To the right of the *Length* column, create a new column entitled *Formula*. In the cell underneath the *Formula* header, copy the following code:

=C2*F2

This simply multiplies the search volume parameter and the keyword length parameter. This isn't useful on its own, but *is* useful as a relative guide when applied to all of the keywords. So as before, from the bottom right-hand corner of the cell, drag this formula to the bottom of the spreadsheet.

Now we need to sort the keywords by these numbers. Click the *Sort & Filter* button in the top right-hand corner, and then *Custom Sort*. Ensure 'My data has headers' is ticked, and select to sort by the *Formula* column. Under 'Order', select 'Largest to Smallest', and click *OK*. You will now notice that some of the long-tail keywords have been pushed more toward the top of the page, which is exactly what we want.

Competing Sites

We've ranked our keywords according to both search volume and keyword length, and we have the beginnings of a workable list. The next step is a little more subjective, and requires us to scan the list from the top down and reject keywords that strike us as being *any* of the following:

1. too competitive (probably by being too short, and with a high search volume)
2. non-commercial (probably by being too general, and being used for those with merely informational [and not transactional] intent, as covered in the earlier *High-Converting Keywords* section detailing the buying cycle)
3. irrelevant (by being suggested by the Google keyword tool, but definitely aren't applicable to our campaign)

To distinguish those keywords you've already reviewed and rejected, it may help to use the Fill Colour button and highlight them red.

Keep going down until you find a suitable, candidate keyword. There are two further steps to determine if this keyword really is worth pursuing, and both strongly relate to search engine optimisation.

Firstly, we want to determine the number of sites that Google says are competing for that keyword. The more there are, the tougher it will be to rank for it successfully. For this, all you need to do is open Google, and search for the keyword in double quotation marks.[8] For example, entering "da vinci biography" (*including* the quotation marks) into Google yields 629,000 competing sites. This sounds a lot, and while it won't be very easy, with a sustained article marketing campaign, it is far from impossible to rank for this keyword on the first page of Google. As a rule of thumb, I rate competing site ranking difficulties as follows:

---

[8] We use quotation marks effectively to do a Phrase match search. If the keyword is entered without quotation marks then we are running a broad search, and Google returns more, less directly competitive sites, which gives a poorer gauge of the competition levels. So when searching for "da vinci biography" without the quotation marks, Google returns 6,770,000 results.

Competing site volume	Ease of Google page one ranking
0–50,000	Easy
50,000–100,000	Medium-Easy
100,000–500,000	Medium
500,000–1,000,000	Medium-Difficult
1,000,000+	Difficult

These are only a guide because many other factors are involved, but this is the first step in helping you to quantify the amount of work it will take to rank for any certain keyword. If there are more than 100,000 competing sites for your chosen keyword, particularly in these early days, you may want to consider selecting another. However, if you have less than 100,000 competing sites, move to the final step: PageRank.

Don't forget to make a note of the competing sites in your spreadsheet. You may find it useful later.

PageRank

For every webpage (i.e. not website), Google assigns a number between 0 and 10, called a PageRank.[9] This number is based on how much Google's algorithms 'like' this page: the genuinely decent content, the originality and the influence it carries. The majority of sites, particularly new ones, have PageRanks of 0 and 1. At the other end of the scale, sites with a PageRank of 10 (or, PR10) are thin on the ground and are the titans of the internet: Microsoft, Apple, Google, Intel, Adobe, NASA, the US government's official site etc.

Of course, Google does not display PageRank information in the normal results page, so we must download and install a plugin called SEOquake, available from www.seoquake.com. Note: you must use either the Chrome or Firefox web browsers for this; it does not work with Internet Explorer.

---

[9] PageRank is named not after the 'page' of the website, but instead after Larry Page, one of the co-founders of Google.

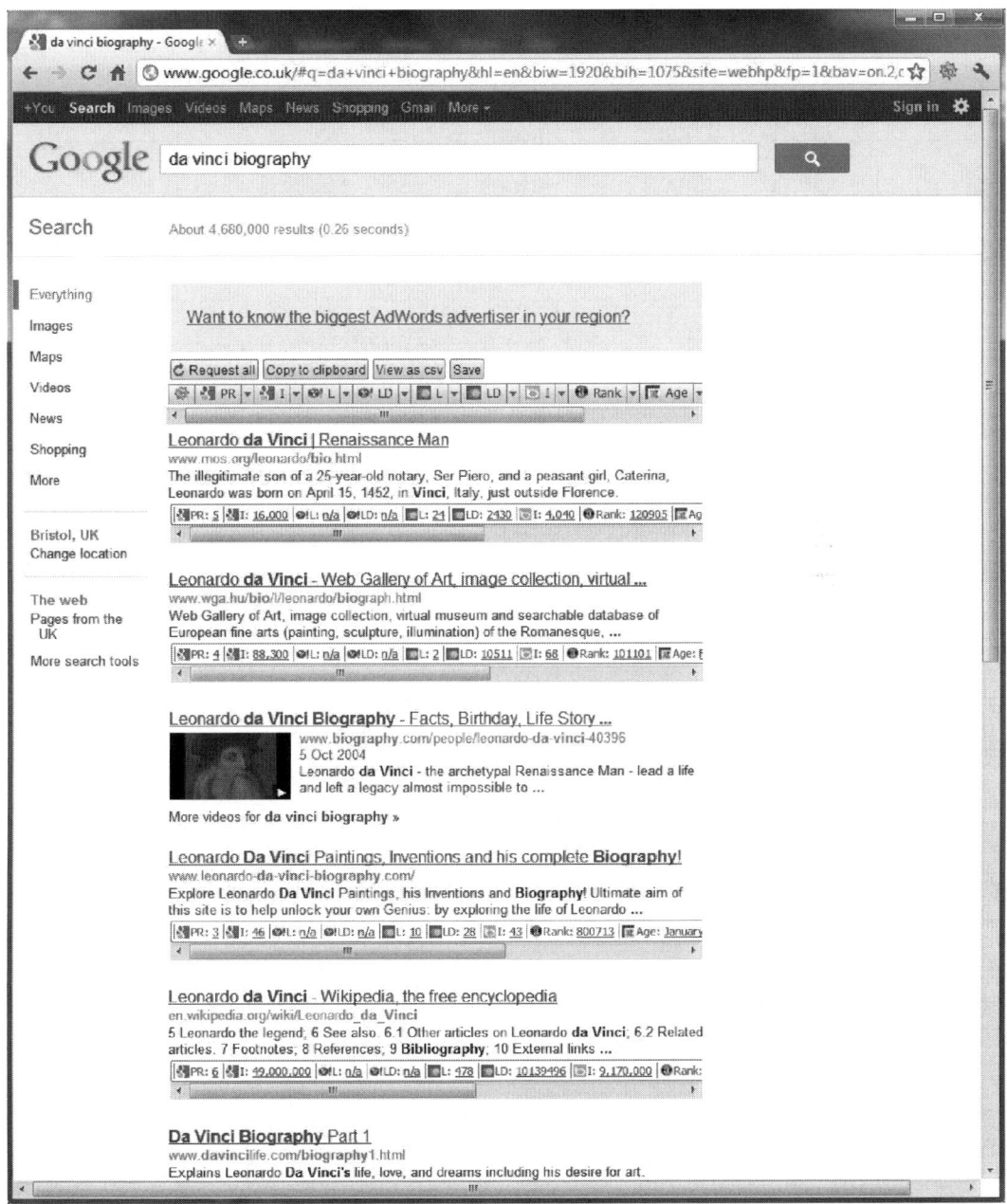

Fig. 19: SEOquake running in Chrome, displaying the Google results page.

Once SEOquake is installed, the task before us is to determine where our competing sites sit on this PageRank scale. Enter the keyword into Google, and if the majority of sites on the first page have PageRanks of around 0 and 1, then we're looking at a useable keyword. If, however, the results include several sites with PageRanks of around 6 or 7, then you'd need to go back to your master keyword list and identify another, because the competition will be overwhelming.

Once installed and enabled, your Google results page will look slightly different, as illustrated in Fig. 19

Notice the new information bar underneath each resulting webpage; at the left-hand side of each one, you'll see the corresponding PR value.

The PageRank values for this particular keyword are as follows: 5, 4, 3, 6, 2, 4, 1, 4, 4. (Notice there are nine results, not ten, as one page was missed by SEOquake.) Therefore, we're facing at least four PR4 pages, a PR5 page and a PR6 page. Not too promising: taking an average of these values, we're looking at an average PageRank of 33/9, or 3.3. This is too competitive for us at the moment, so in this case we'll make a note of this figure in our spreadsheet and return to our master keyword list.

As for the specifics of how difficult it will be to rank for a specific keyword based on its average PageRank, use the following guide:

Average PageRank	Ease of Google page one ranking
0–1.5	Easy
1.5–2.0	Medium-Easy
2.0–2.5	Medium
2.5–3.0	Medium-Difficult
3.0+	Difficult

With practice, it doesn't take long to determine both the number of competing sites and the PageRank values of each keyword, so don't worry about analysing several keywords until you find one that measures up. Remember that it's worth investing some time to identify strong keywords, as this is what all the work was for leading up to this point.

For example, after some further analysis, 'leonardo da vinci facts' has 8,100 searches per month and a much lower average PageRank of 2.33, which could be used to drive traffic to a page with related content. If you're looking to sell related products, 'last supper poster' has 590 monthly searches, which is acceptable, and an even lower average PageRank of 1.9.

In total, I recommend identifying at least six keywords you can use in your various marketing campaigns. One of the most powerful methods through which you can now apply your keywords is article marketing, which is explored in Part II.

4 Advanced Techniques and Sources of Keywords

These methods and considerations are entirely optional, and have been included for more experienced marketers and/or those of a more technical disposition.

Competing Websites   **Difficulty ●●●●●**

There is a straightforward way to capture the keywords that your competitors are using. You could define the competition as both (A) the sites that are ranking highly for your keyword in Google as well as (B) known, specific companies you wish to dominate in the SERPs. Both groups potentially contain many hidden keywords that are easy to discover. If you wish to expand your keyword list, strongly consider using this method for its power and simplicity.

Open the Google AdWords Keyword Tool - don't forget to sign in and select 'Exact' or 'Phrase' match *and* deselect 'Broad'.

Underneath the 'Word or phrase' field is a 'Website' field into which you can copy and paste the address of any webpage you wish to analyse. For example, at the top of the SERPs for 'da vinci' is the Wikipedia entry. Leaving the 'Word or phrase' field empty, paste the full URL 'http://en.wikipedia.org/wiki/Leonardo_da_Vinci' into the 'Website' field and hit *Search*. Many new keywords are suggested, and once saved are easily appended to your existing list.

Don't forget to run the competition's website pages through the tool too, although don't stop at just the home page (or front/main page). Remember the tool only checks pages, not complete sites, so analyse any and all pages of interest such as About pages or Product pages. Don't worry about duplicating keywords, as they can be easily removed as described previously. The CSV files you create here can simply be added to your Keyword folder. To keep track of those webpages that you have already analysed, name your CSV file accordingly.

Sitemaps   **Difficulty** ●●●●●

This is a natural and optional follow-on, insomuch as it may help you to compile a list of webpages that are worth running through the Google keyword tool, by listing the specific pages within a website that could be analysed, such as your competitor's.

Most websites possess what is known as a 'sitemap', which is an XML file that helps search engines understand and index the pages of a website.

Using an example site, www.taichi-exercises.com, the sitemap is usually located in the same relative location at the end, i.e. www.taichi-exercises.com/sitemap.xml.

There are two ways to discover the pages within a website, and the choice between them purely boils down to preference:

- Option #1: Open Google and enter 'site:www.taichi-exercises.com' (replacing the website with one of your choosing). This returns all the pages Google has indexed for this site.
- Option #2: Open Excel, and then open the *Data* tab. Click on the *From Other Sources* button, and select *From XML Data Import*. In the *File name* field, enter the full location of the sitemap (including the 'http://' part), e.g. http://www.taichi-exercises.com/sitemap.xml, and hit *Open*. Excel then takes a moment to import the page listings.

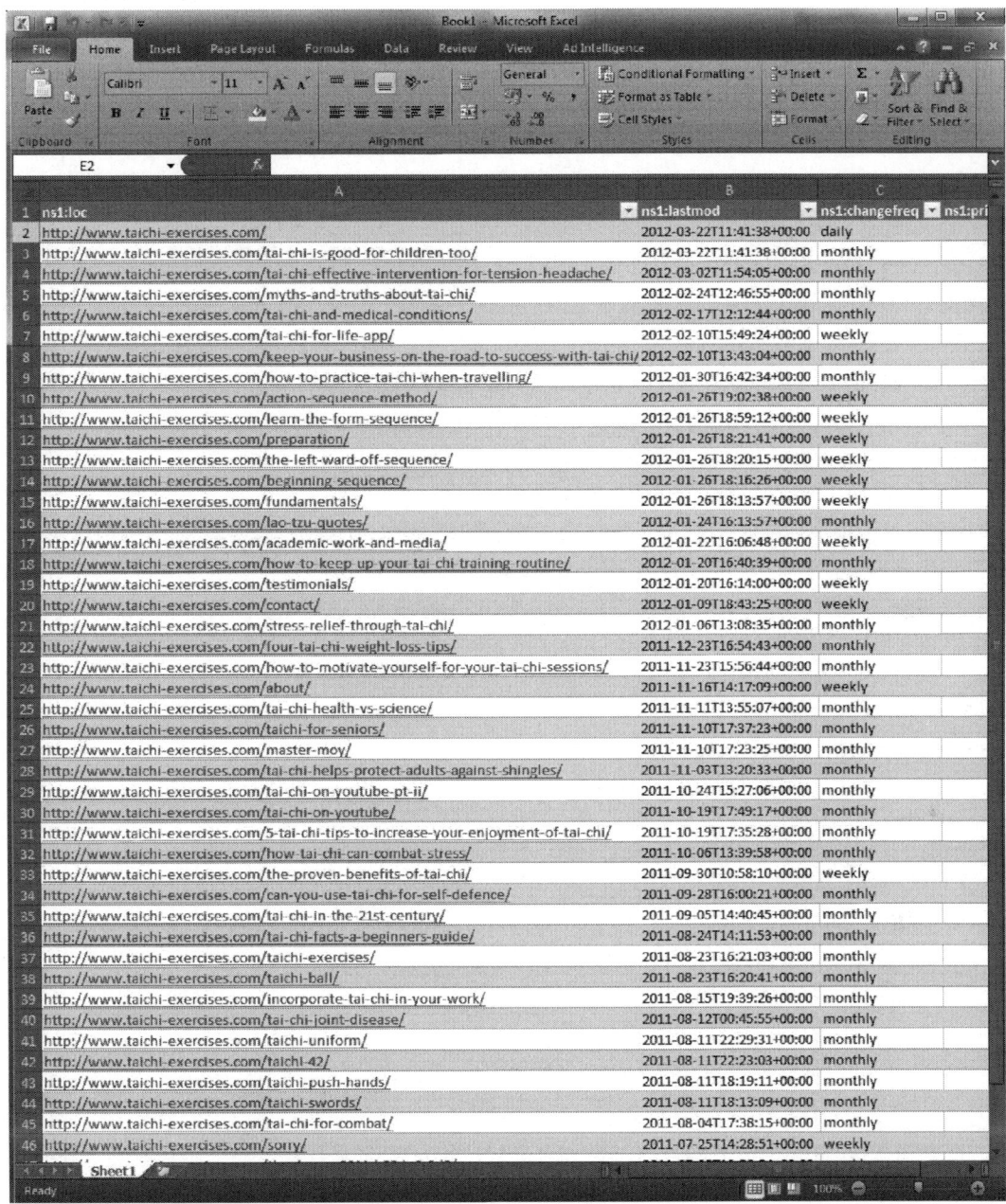

Fig. 20: Excel after importing the sitemap data from www.taichi-exercises.com.

Ultimately, try to target pages that are likely to be relevant and keyword-rich. For example, avoid analysing Privacy Policy or Terms & Conditions pages.

Google Analytics   **Difficulty** ●●●●●

If you currently don't have Google Analytics installed on your site, I highly recommend you do so now (from www.google.com/analytics). It captures very useful data about your visitors – not only the keywords they used to reach your site, but also the pages they landed on, bounce rates, demographic data and even the browser they used. A compelling reason to install it ASAP is that data can only be pulled from the moment the code is installed on your site; it cannot be pulled retroactively.

The first thing Google does is confirm you're the site owner by asking you to insert a unique line of code in the HTML of your website. Once this step is done, Google begins recording traffic activity. Once it has been running long enough to gather some useful data, log into Google Analytics and head to the following page:

> Traffic Sources → Sources → Search → Organic

You can now view up to 500 valuable keywords that undisputedly drove traffic to your site. You can export these to a CSV file for future reference (using the Export button at the top), but these can't be added into your Keywords folder because the files are laid out differently, and, therefore, can't be merged. You must instead run each keyword of interest through the Google keyword tool and then save the results to the Keywords folder: this method, in turn, generates more keywords.

Google Site Search   **Difficulty** ●●●●●

You've probably seen sites that have a search box of their own for internal site searches. These only return results from that particular site and don't include general internet-wide searches.

One such way to add this functionality to your own site is to install Google Site Search (from www.google.com/sitesearch). Once enabled, this allows you to capture data on the keywords visitors use when actually on your site: this offers a unique insight into what they expect to see and hope to find there. If you discover any recurring keywords, it's a good idea to create some genuinely useful content to satisfy the expectations of those searching for it.

Again, any new keywords of interest should be run through the Google keyword tool and saved in the Keywords folder.

Note: this is a paid service, starting with a $100 annual fee based on a 20,000 search query limit.

Google Autocomplete   Difficulty ●●●●●

If it's enabled in your browser (or when using Google directly), you will notice that when typing in a search phrase, your search engine of choice begins to make educated guesses at the full search term you wish to enter. This is known as Google Autocomplete (or Google Suggest) and offers another cornucopia of keyword ideas.

Firefox is the best tool for this, serving up ten suggestions underneath the search box. Type in your root keyword and instantly see longer keywords appear underneath. You can dig further by typing '*root keyword* a' to view suggested keywords that begin with an 'a', and then '*root keyword* b' to do the same with keywords that begin with a 'b'. Continue alphabetically, identifying any potentially valuable keywords and running them individually through the Google keyword tool and saving the results. Remember that keywords should be relevant, and if driving traffic to, say, a sales letter, the keyword should be a term that someone toward the end of the buying cycle would use.

This process can be semi-automated by using http://ubersuggest.org. Enter your root keyword, select the language and hit *Suggest*. The tool then systematically processes the Google Autocomplete results, which is a massive timesaver.

Note: Google Autocomplete isn't the same as Google Instant, which is where Google dynamically updates its results pages while you type your search term.

Microsoft Advertising Intelligence   **Difficulty ●●●○○**

For some time, Microsoft ran the *Online Commercial Intent* tool (now permanently unavailable), which attempted to attach commercial values for each keyword between 0 and 1. If someone entered a particular keyword into a search engine, what level of confidence could you have that if they landed on your site, their intention would be to spend money on your products or services? This tool made an effort to quantify that possibility.

This tool was replaced and upgraded by the Microsoft *Advertising Intelligence* tool, which can be downloaded from http://adlab.microsoft.com. There are two prerequisites: you must have Excel 2007 or Excel 2010 installed, and if you don't have an adCenter account, you will need to create one at https://adcenter.microsoft.com. For maximum compatibility, use Internet Explorer while creating an account.

Once installed and configured (you will need to enter your account details, albeit just once, to run it) in Excel, the tool pulls keyword data from searches entered into Bing, which can include additional data, such as monthly traffic forecasts and monetisation KPIs (key performance indicators), such as clickthrough rates. This adds another dimension to your research, because it's now possible to identify keywords that are actively clicked on, rather than just passively viewed.

Start with the *Keyword Wizard*, which is the first button in the new Ad Intelligence tab.

1. Select 'Excel range' and then *Next*. Type your root keywords, and then click *Next* twice.
2. Select both the 'Campaign association' and 'Queries That Contain Your Keyword' boxes, and then *Next*. Increase the maximum number of suggested keywords to 100 for both of these, and click *Next* twice.
3. Select both 'Monthly traffic' and 'Monetization', and continue clicking *Next* until it greys out and you must click *Finish*.

Excel contacts its databases and imports the keyword data right into Excel. You can now filter and sort it based on not only search volume, but also any perceived trends and CTR information. Any keywords identified should be run through the Google keyword tool and saved into the Keywords folder.

Misspellings   Difficulty ●●●●●

During your keyword research, you will undoubtedly come across misspelt variations, which in short I recommend avoiding, even if they have encouraging metrics in terms of search volume and competition.

Keywords can be applied either visibly (in articles, webpage titles, anchor text etc.) or invisibly (meta tags). As the majority of methods involve using your keywords visibly, this means you will have to use them prominently. This goes beyond keeping search engines happy: once your site gains traction and receives traffic, authority and professional credibility will take a nosedive if your site is peppered with misspellings. Bounce rates will increase, and rankings will inevitably fall.

In the end, including misspellings in your copy or website is not a serious or long-term solution.

Keyword Derivations   Difficulty ●●●●●

Another way to broaden your root keyword is to consider it as a stem for longer variations. In other words, from the root keyword (example, 'read'), further keywords can be derived by adding prefixes ('*mis*read') and suffixes ('read*able*').

This can be done quite easily using a tool such as this one:

www.usingenglish.com/resources/wordcheck

Enter your root keyword, hit *Check* and click the link underneath 'Similar Words' at the bottom.

For example, if you were researching the phrase 'investment strategy', you could look at both words for possible alternatives.

'invest' prefixes: disinvest, overinvest, reinvest, uninvest.

'invest' suffixes: investable, invested, investible, investigatable, investigate, investigated, investigates, investigating, investigation, investigational, investigations, investigative, investigator, investigators, investigatory, investing, investitive, investiture, investitures, investment, investments, investor, investors, invests.

'strategy' suffixes: strategic, strategically, strategics, strategies, strategist, strategists.

Note that not all are relevant, but that was expected. It doesn't take long to identify those that could, however, be run through the Google keyword tool. Remember, no two keywords have the same metrics.

Of course, the simplest way to experiment with root keyword variations is to run its plural form through the Google keyword tool. So if you're promoting a detached property in Edinburgh, don't forget to process both 'Edinburgh detached property' and 'Edinburgh detached properties'. Both will yield different search volumes and competing site PageRanks.

Direct Surveys   Difficulty ●●○○○

If you have access to a mailing list or other respectably sized group of people (e.g. Facebook or Twitter), you can ask them directly what phrases they would use to search when given a predefined situation.

It's free to use SurveyMonkey (www.surveymonkey.com) to send 10 questions (and receive up to 100 responses) in a survey to your contacts, and it captures and compiles the results into a clearly understood report. Surveys also come in handy because you can ask your clients what their perceptions and preconceptions are of your products or

services, and any questions or even any doubts they may have. This knowledge is all valuable ammunition when writing sales copy or FAQs for your site. You could also begin collecting market data: how much would they be prepared to pay? Are those who are interested predominantly male or female?

Forums

Difficulty ●●●●●

One way to gather keywords used by your target market is in active market (or niche-specific) forums. Just search in Google for [*keyword* "forum"], with the double quotation marks, and *without* the brackets.[10] You can then run pages from the forums you identify through the Google AdWords Keyword Tool, as well as scanning through the pages with your own eyes for anything striking you as a keyword (or even better, reoccurring keywords) that a buyer would use.

Searching through forums has a secondary benefit. As you begin to familiarise yourself with who your buyers are, you also begin the process of market segmentation. You can define several crucial characteristics of your market: marital status, age, perhaps how close they are to retirement, the number of children they have, discretionary income, lifestyle interests, personality, location, how tech-savvy they are, etc.

This information is useful at every step of new product development. Idea screening, pricing, copywriting – the product is laser-targeted at a well-defined group of individuals. You can then embody all these characteristics into a person you can visualise, called a *persona*. Give the person a name, age, background, motivations, goals and a personality. Ask them questions and imagine what their answer would be, using the context of this person's 'real' life. In short, this adds a subjective, human element to the more objective segmentation data. Ultimately, this means you can build and optimise your website design and sales copy around the very type of people who can connect and relate to your service.

---

[10] With the advent of Google+ (Google's venture into social networking), the '+' sign search operator (that forces Google to include a certain term in the SERPs) was dropped and replaced with double quotation marks.

Tag Clouds

Difficulty ●●●●●

On some sites, clouds of keywords can be seen that give a quick representation of words or topics used throughout. These words are occasionally hyperlinked to relevant onsite content. Additionally, they are occasionally weighted by font size to visualise word frequency – terms that are more popular are displayed in a larger font.

These won't be a primary source of keyword ideas, but if during your research you come across one, say on a competing website, scan through it to identify any terms worthy of further investigation.

Server Logs

Difficulty ●●●●●

The specifics of how to perform this are highly advanced and beyond the scope of this book, but if you're a site owner, your web server stores referral data from site visitors, including the keywords they used to reach you. This is obviously valuable information, but you'll require the right toolset to pull it from your server logs. One such tool is AWStats (http://awstats.sourceforge.net), which is free. However, Perl is required to run AWStats. If you run a Linux server, it's probably already installed. If you run a Windows server, you can download ActivePerl, again for free, from www.activestate.com/activeperl/downloads.

Google announced in October 2011[11] that they would be rolling out encrypted search as standard. In the browser's address bar, the difference appears minimal: http://www.google.co.uk becomes https://www.google.co.uk. The additional 's' is because the connection to Google is now protected by a security protocol named Secure Sockets Layer (SSL), and referral data is now *not* forwarded to, or intercepted by, third parties. This increased privacy is good news for consumers, but bad news for marketers who use this information to learn which keywords drive their users to their site. Note: this only applies to *organic* searches from Google – paid searches (i.e. PPC)

---

[11] http://googleblog.blogspot.com/2011/10/making-search-more-secure.html

will continue to receive referral data. In addition, if you're the owner of an encrypted site, Google will again oblige and forward you secure keyword data.

Google Search Operators

Search operators are simple instructions you can give Google when running a search. These can be quite useful when narrowing down your list of keywords because they help to differentiate between those sites that merely contain your keyword (or broad interpretations of it) and those which the site owner is, in all likelihood, actively targeting and with whom you're directly competing. The three most commonly used search operators are the following:

1. Intitle

Definition: This operator returns pages that contain the keyword in the title tag.

Example usage in Google: *intitle:"da vinci"*

Example result: www.bbc.co.uk/science/leonardo

This page is returned because the title reads: 'BBC Science | Learn about Leonardo **da Vinci**'.

2. Inanchor

Definition: This operator returns pages that have links to them that contain the keyword in the anchor text.

Example usage in Google: *inanchor:"da vinci"*

Example result: en.wikipedia.org/wiki/Leonardo_da_Vinci

This page is returned because there will be many inbound links that use the wording '**Da Vinci**' in the anchor text back to that page.

3. Inurl

Definition: This operator returns pages that actually contain the keyword in the URL, i.e. not just the main site copy. So this locates articles that have been written directly about the keyword you're scrutinising.

Example usage in Google: *inurl:"da vinci"*

Example result: www.guardian.co.uk/artanddesign/.../2011/.../lost-**da**-**vinci**-mystery

Operator Combinations

You may also combine these operators in a single search. For example, you could use the following search phrase:

inurl:"da vinci" intitle:"da vinci"

This will return all pages that contain "da vinci" in the URL *and* the page title.

In terms of priority, *inurl* is probably the least revealing of the three, because it's perfectly possible to create a compelling page (in Google's eyes) without necessarily including the keyword in the URL. The title tag and incoming anchor text results are stronger gauges of the direct competition.

Ordinarily, you would have to capture this information one keyword at a time. There is, however, a free tool that automates the analysis of keywords in this way at http://eugie17.hubpages.com/hub/Keyword-Competition-Tool-for-SEO-analysis. This tool returns the results of pages that include all three of these operators: *intitle*, *inanchor* and *inurl*. Note: this tool requires Java to be installed.

The ~ Operator

The final Google operator worth knowing is called the ~ (tilde) operator, or synonym operator. This does an effective job of suggesting alternative words as part of the search, as well as including suffixes to the keyword to which you apply it.

By way of example, entering '~backpack' (note: there is no space between the operator and the word) not only returns results including 'backpack', but also 'backpacking', 'luggage', 'bags' and 'camping'. This is a quick and easy way to expand your keyword list.

Keyword Effectiveness Index

If you haven't come across it before, the Keyword Effectiveness Index (KEI) is promoted as a useful metric in gauging the relative value of each keyword in a list. The exact formula tends to differ depending on where you read it, but the simpler definition is accepted to be:

$$KEI = \frac{\text{Monthly Searches}}{\text{Competing Sites}}$$

What is missing are metrics that cover basic commerciality (i.e. keyphrase length – generally, the longer the better) and the difficulty of ranking for that particular keyword in the SERPs (i.e. PageRank data). Therefore, in my opinion, it's quite basic and incomplete, and on its own it should only be a tertiary consideration in which keywords to target.

As a side note, we can create a much better, 'unofficial' KEI (let's call it Mason's KEI) from the data in our master keyword list, using a function in Excel:

$$KEI = \frac{\text{Monthly Searches} \times \text{Keyword Length}}{\text{Competing Sites} \times \text{Average PageRank}}$$

Together, these parameters combine to give a much more powerful relative value to each keyword. A formula can easily be created in Excel and applied to each keyword in a new column, and then the keywords can be sorted by the values in this column, large to small. This begins to sort your keywords in order of commercial and good ranking potential.

Automation

It's worth mentioning that there are many keyword-specific SEO tools, which range from free to enterprise-level that cost $500+ per month. The cost varies depending on how much data is pulled, and the 'purity' of that data, which is dependent on the source (Browser toolbars and ISP data are but two other sources, aside from data compiled directly by search engines). Specific tools are listed for reference in the Appendix.

One specific piece of software I would like to mention and recommend is the Keyword Advantage tool, available from the Niche Profit Classroom at www.nicheprofitclassroom.com. This does an outstanding job of automating the 'data gathering' phase of your keyword research. Once keywords are identified with the Google AdWords Keyword Tool, these can be fed *en masse* through the Keyword Advantage tool, which captures competing site and average PageRank data.

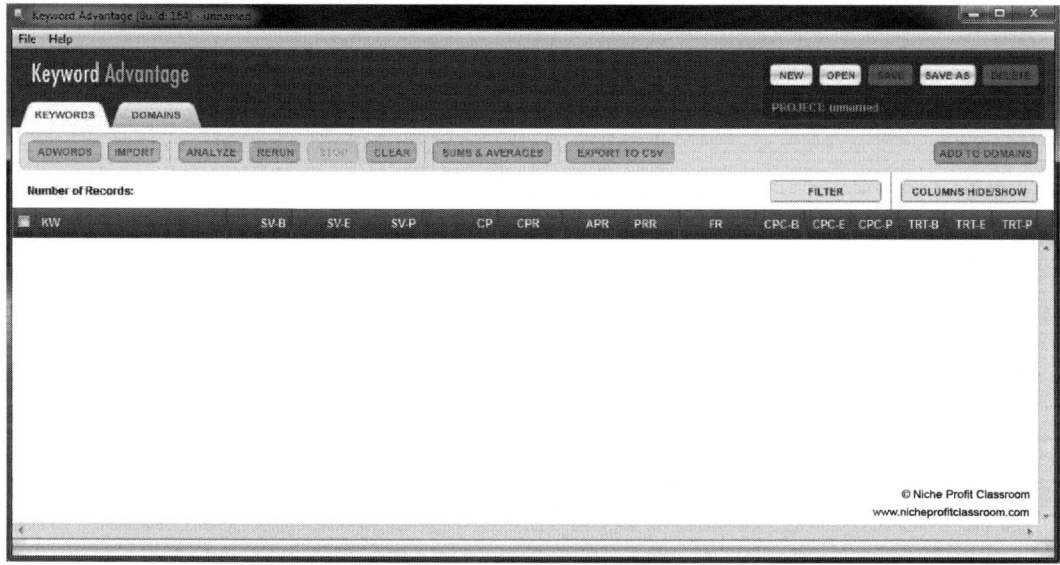

Fig. 21: The Keyword Advantage tool interface.

Once several hundred (or even several thousand) keywords are imported into the tool, it can be run overnight with fresh competition data awaiting you in the morning. This enables you to populate a large spreadsheet with an awful lot of valuable, first-hand information with little effort. Results can then be exported and sorted in Excel.

As a bonus feature, domains can also be checked for availability, based on your keywords. To paraphrase, each keyword is checked for the equivalent .com, .org and .net domain to see whether you can register them (or if they have already been registered and are unavailable). If you're working on a new project, this information is part and parcel of which keywords to target.

Note: the Keyword Advantage tool is currently Windows only. If you're an Intel-based Mac user, you have to run virtual machine (VM) software such as *Parallels Desktop for Mac* or *VMware Fusion*.

5 Local and Mobile Search

Local Search

One way to enhance and refine your keywords is to cater for searches applied to your locality, town or county, depending on your service area. This should be of interest to local businesses, which in most cases will have competition to outmanoeuvre in the search engine rankings.

Several tools exist that can assist in collecting local search data.

Keyword List Generator

➜ http://tools.seobook.com/keyword-list/generator.php

This is an easy way to manually create a list of keywords that feature your business and local place names. Enter variations, plurals and synonyms of your business in the *Word List* boxes, and hit *Generate*. For example, enter the following into the respective boxes:

Word List 1: PC,computer

Word List 2: repair,repairs

Word List 3: helmsley,york,yorkshire

They are then combined into the following keyword list:

"PC repair helmsley"   "PC repair york"   "PC repair yorkshire"

"PC repairs helmsley"

"PC repairs york"

"PC repairs yorkshire"

"computer repair helmsley"

"computer repair york"

"computer repair yorkshire"

"computer repairs helmsley"

"computer repairs york"

"computer repairs yorkshire"

These can be entered into the Google keyword tool *simultaneously* (one per line in the *Word or phrase* field), and search data captured: "computer repair york" has 390 Phrase match searches per month and is the clear leader.

This can be taken further, because, don't forget, it's in Google's nature to suggest alternative keywords. Now, inserting the three example location place names in the *Include terms* box on the left-hand side of the tool, and manually excluding irrelevant results, we discover that "york computer repair" has 480 monthly searches. Competition data aside, already we have two promising keywords worth further investigation, and equally as important, we know which keywords *not* to waste time trying to target.

UK Postcode Radius Search Map

➔ www.freemaptools.com/find-uk-postcodes-inside-radius.htm

This allows you to compile postcodes within a radius of your service area, and again these can be anaysed to see which are searched most frequently, and added to your company's service area page. For instance, following the steps in the tool, we can identify the postcodes within 25km of Helmsley to be TS9, YO17, YO18, YO60, YO61, YO62, and YO7. All this will help feed Google the information necessary for it to understand the areas your business serves.

GeoNames

→ www.geonames.org

Lastly, this tool quickly identifies local towns that again could be included in your website content.

The interface is straightforward: enter the town of interest and hit *Search*. In the next window, I recommend unselecting all tickboxes under the *Features* box, except for the first category ('city, village'). Consequently, it doesn't take long to generate a list of towns automatically, in this case within 20km of Helmsley:

Kirby Misperton	Nawton	Scawton	Carlton
Kirby Knowle	Kirkbymoorside	Great Edston	Welburn
Harome	Cold Kirby	Felixkirk	Upsall
Thirlby	Old Byland	Cawthorn	Hutton le Hole
Boltby	Nunnington	Bagby	Normanby
Oswaldkirk	Wass	Salton	Sutton
Marton	Rievaulx	Middleton	Woolmoor
Appleton le Moors	Thirsk	Sinnington	

This is useful when applied in conjunction with the Keyword List Generator to identify keyphrases with relatively high local search volumes. In addition, this is useful because if you're a local or regional business (rather than national or international), keyword competition levels tend to be much more manageable.

Native-Language Vocabulary

Be wary of local slang and colloquialisms if you're actively targeting an unfamiliar area. You may want to optimise your keywords for the regional vernacular.

For example, if you're selling shoes (online or offline), remember that plimsoll shoes aren't called plimsoll shoes everywhere on the planet. In English-speaking countries alone they're variously referred to as plimsoles, sannies, gutties, daps, dappers, pumps, sneakers, tennis shoes, deck shoes, sandshoes, canvas shoes, tekkies and tackies. Optimising for the wrong word or phrase in a local market could be highly unproductive; a little research, perhaps with a native speaker, could go a long way.

Also bear in mind that any one country doesn't limit itself to a single language. In the UK alone, there are *eight* living indigenous languages in addition to English, including Scots, Welsh and Irish. There are also many immigrant languages, including Punjabi, Bengali and Urdu. This may open up some less competitive options for you, depending on your products or services.

Listings

There are now many online services that offer free business listings.

To get started, ensure you complete a listing for your business on Google Places (www.google.com/local/add/businessCenter). Once you are verified as the owner, basic details such as your business address and telephone number can be entered, as well as extended information such as your service area, opening hours, website, a 200-character short description, photos, and even business videos you may have posted on YouTube.

Bing also has a listing service, which can be completed via www.bing.com/businessportal if you're based in the US, or alternatively via http://marketlocation.my118information.co.uk if you're based in the UK.

Finally, GetListed.org (http://uk.getlisted.org) is a tool that checks your online presence against many listing directories, including Yelp and Global Brownbook, and offers suggestions on how to improve your content in those directories, including adding reviews of your business.

Mobile Search

It's important to consider the rise of mobile search in recent years: people are no longer confined to their desktops and laptops to run a search for a local business. Looking at the market share, mobile searches represented 3.92% of all searches in March 2011. By January 2012, that figure had more than doubled to 8.77%.[12] Moreover, Google maintains a mighty 97% share of that mobile search engine market.[13]

As of January 2012, the iPad was the most heavily used mobile device for search. Android devices and iPhones followed closely behind.[14] This device data is useful when deciding which screen resolutions you must work around.

This all happened so fast due to a phenomenon known as technological convergence. It's not just that smartphones became faster; there has also been serious development into touchscreens, geolocation technology, mapping technology, 3G and wifi hotspot coverage when out and about, fast wireless access points in the office, fibre optic broadband at home, online payment systems, and the power and commerciality of apps. In addition, we won't have to wait too long until 4G, the successor to 3G, is rolled out. In short, mobile search will only continue to accelerate.

As recently as December 15, 2011, Google upgraded their own bots with a dedicated one (cunningly named 'Googlebot-Mobile') that crawls through smartphone-specific content.[15]

Because mobile devices generally lack the grunt and screen real estate of desktop PCs, mobile sites are considerably lighter on images and quicker to load. Creating a mobile-friendly site does require a major interface design rethink: Flash shouldn't be used (as it is now only minimally supported by mobile devices, and Adobe has officially ceased

---

[12] http://netmarketshare.com/mobile-market-share?qprid=61
[13] http://gs.statcounter.com
[14] http://www.w3schools.com/browsers/browsers_mobile.asp
[15] http://googlewebmastercentral.blogspot.com/2011/12/introducing-smartphone-googlebot-mobile.html

mobile Flash development), and remember that your users lack a mouse and instead rely on a touchscreen.

However, we are interested in the keywords that users of mobile search are using. Once again, the Google AdWords Keyword Tool comes to our aid.

Open up the *Advanced Options and Filters* options, in which you will find a dropdown menu next to 'Show Ideas and Statistics for', and select 'Mobile devices with full internet browsers'. Google currently considers the following to be full browsers:[16]

- Safari on Apple iPhone, iPod Touch, and iPad
- Android (the native web browser that comes with the device), including Kindle Fire
- Palm webOS (native browser)
- Nokia Maemo (native browser)
- Blackberry 6 (native browser)
- Windows Phone 7.5 (native browser)

Therefore, it's quite straightforward to source a wealth of information specifically inputted into these devices. Don't forget to select the 'Phrase' or 'Exact' match type on the left-hand side of the page. Then apply your knowledge of keyword research to this data: find relevant, specific keywords with relatively high search volume and low competition.

While we're discussing mobile search, it's no surprise that many major retailers have developed standalone mobile apps as an additional (and lucrative) sales channel. Asda, Argos, Next, River Island, Topshop, Tesco and John Lewis all have a presence in the Apple App Store, and offer, more or less, full access to their respective catalogues. The Amazon Mobile app goes one step further, and offers a direct price comparison facility by allowing the user to scan product barcodes in real-time. It then cross-references this exact product against its own prices to see if they can beat it. This makes full, innovative use of the modern smartphone's capabilities to out-do the competition. As Amazon is currently the UK's largest online retailer, and has been for several years, I'd suggest that they must be doing something right.

---

[16] http://support.google.com/adwords/bin/answer.py?hl=en&answer=107264

Now we have aggregated, analysed and cherry-picked a handful of highly promising keywords, we now move from the research phase into implementation.

6 Applications of Keyword Research

After your research, there are two categories of how and where you can begin to apply them: on your site (*on-page optimisation*) and on other people's sites (*off-page optimisation*). They are both of equally high importance, and both need some degree of action to be taken for Google to take a shine to your site.

On-Page Optimisation

Domain

As discussed previously in the 'Benefits of Keyword Research' section, if you're starting a new website, good keywords can be used to identify an available *exact match domain* such as www.ExactKeyword.com. Use www.godaddy.com to check a domain, and register it if it's available. An exact match domain isn't critical, however, and a *keyword rich domain* using stop words at the end is a worthy alternative, e.g. www.ExactKeywordInfo.com.

Page URLs

This is another practical way to gain leverage from your keywords, and a natural extension from using the keyword in the domain. It gives your site a framework to work around; following your keyword research, you should be able to categorise specific keywords into more general groupings. For example, several keywords apply explicitly to da Vinci's paintings, and this can form a new group, under which relevant articles can be posted using a simple website folder structure:

www.ExampleDaVinciSite.com/da-vinci-paintings/da-vinci-portrait.htm

So now, we have relevant keywords in the domain, and in the URL under both the folder/category name and the name of the page. Contrast this against:

www.ExampleDaVinciSite.com/html/1.htm

You can see how little by little, we're fleshing out the site and page descriptions that search engines can hook into, and we want to make it as easy as possible for them to do so.

Image Optimisation

When you run a search on Google, you may have noticed that it's not uncommon for images to appear at the top of the results page. In many ways, Google is insanely clever, but it does have some difficulty understanding image content. This is where it's a very good idea to help Google, as you can drive traffic to your site from an easily overlooked direction: the images on your site.

Most WYSIWYG (What You See Is What You Get) HTML editors (such as Adobe Dreamweaver) or content management systems (such as WordPress) allow you to edit the image tag. Delegate this to a web builder if you get stuck. There are two common attributes in the image tag we need to look at: *src* and *alt*.

> **<img src="da-vinci-portrait.jpg" alt="A portrait of Leonardo da Vinci in red chalk" height="100" width="100" />**

The *src* attribute tells the browser the location of the image on the server, and naturally must include the file name. Therefore, if the name of your image is *2LqqP1Zba1q.jpg* or *image2.jpg*, Google has very little with which to work. However, naming it something like *da-vinci-portrait.jpg*, enables it to become much clearer for the search engines.

The *alt* attribute is a string of descriptive text you're allowed to use if for whatever reason the image doesn't display. In this case, don't just use the raw keyword; instead, integrate it (once only) or a closely similar keyword into a short, objective, readable sentence of what the image is.

Page Titles

From Google's official Webmaster Central Blog:

> *"Page titles are an important part of our search results: they're the first line of each result and they're the actual links our searchers click to reach websites."*[17]

If Google says page titles are important, it's wise to listen. These short descriptions appear at the top of the browser and, more importantly, offer Google (as well as the end user) a short, powerful declaration about the content of the page. This is the HTML code:

<title>Da Vinci | Da Vinci Paintings</title>

Keep these short, say 60 characters tops, and include your keyword (or a similar variation). A common format is to have your root keyword followed by your longer-tail keyword, separated by a vertical bar (or 'pipe'), for example:

PC Repair | Computer and Laptop Repair Services

T'ai Chi Exercises | Lao Tzu Quotes from his Tao Te Ching

Description Meta Tag

This is a longer description of the webpage content, written in original, clear prose (not a disjointed sequence of keywords), although still kept under 160 characters. Although, of course, you should still use your keyword (or variation thereof) in this text. Along

---

[17] http://googlewebmastercentral.blogspot.com/2012/01/better-page-titles-in-search-results.html

with page titles, this is another important opportunity to explain to search engines *and* potential site visitors what your page offers them. This is the HTML:

> **<meta name="description" content="This da Vinci self-portrait, created c.1512, was drawn on paper with red chalk. Although some argue that the subject isn't in fact da Vinci, but someone else." />**

In what is a small venture into copywriting, as your description is generally presented directly in the SERPs, try to end the description with a small cliffhanger to make the reader feel *compelled* to click on the link.

Keyword Meta Tag

There is a dedicated meta tag for keywords within your webpage. Ironically, this is probably the one to which you want to pay least attention, as most search engines do a brilliant job of disregarding them. This can be swiftly blamed by their abuse in the earlier years of the internet: keywords were rammed into here *en masse*, and while search engines were still in their infancy and more easily manipulated, these keyword meta tags led them astray and rewarded sites of dubious content.

Nowadays it's other way around, as no one would use a search engine that is easily tricked and serves up second-rate results. Unique, valuable content is rewarded, not an overexploited area to 'dump' keywords. You have nothing to lose by including a couple of keywords in this field; it's just that realistically you don't have a terrific amount to gain, either. Purely for reference, here is an example piece of HTML:

> **<meta name="keywords" content="da vinci self portrait, leonardo da vinci self portrait, da vinci portrait, leonardo da vinci portrait, da vinci portraits, leonardo da vinci portraits, portrait of leonardo da vinci, portrait leonardo da vinci, self portrait of leonardo da vinci, self portrait leonardo da vinci" />**

Internal Link Anchor Text

When one thinks of links, don't deal exclusively with inbound links: remember that Google also tries to understand the content of your site by looking at how pages link internally to each other.

Use keywords as your anchor text on such links. So on one of your pages you may have 'Read more on da Vinci's Vitruvian Man <u>here</u>'. However, 'here' as a keyword tells search engines nothing about the page to which it is linking. However, a simple amendment to 'Read more on da Vinci's <u>Vitruvian Man</u>' is something Google can latch onto, and improves your chances of ranking well for that keyword.

Off-Page Optimisation

Article Marketing

As will be explained in detail in the next section, there are many reasons to do article marketing subsequent to the keyword research. Articles are 500-word, non-promotional, informative, unique pieces of content that are distributed on the internet, most often to dedicated article directories, although there are other places to post them.

Each article is prepared for a single keyword: some get greedy and purposefully try to stuff the article with several keywords, or overdo the same keyword. The keyword is also inserted into a small, but important, section at the end, which *is* promotional. Use a professional article distribution service (such as Submit Your Article – <u>www.submityourarticle.com</u>) and your webpage(s) will benefit from many backlinks, as well as many other benefits. This is covered in more detail in *Chapter 8: Benefits of Article Marketing*.

Forum Participation

In the same way that you can set a 'signature block' that is automatically appended to the bottom of every email, you can set a signature within the account/admin settings of most forums.

Google [*keyword* "forum"] with the quotation marks, and without the brackets, to identify the forums in your niche. Moreover, not just any forum: find active forums with high numbers of users (good forums report the numbers of currently active users they have in the information at the bottom).

Getting involved is key: answer questions, give meaningful replies, raise interesting topics and post recent developments, all with no hard selling. Become the authority. And for each post or reply you submit, your signature at the bottom contains a link (with your keyword as the anchor text) back to your site. Both search engines and forum users see these links, which helps your site to be indexed *and* drives targeted traffic to your site.

Blog Comments

Very similar to contributing to a forum, this method involves commenting on blogs. Blogs can be personal, or belong to a company. The important thing is to add genuinely valuable content: expect generic comments along the lines of 'great post!' or 'visit my site!' to be promptly deleted. Genuinely engage with the blog post; perhaps offer a constructive counterargument, or outline some relevant, informative experience you had on the topic.

Again, Google will eventually pick up an understated, unobtrusive link at the bottom of your comment, which either contains an HTML link with the keyword as the anchor text, or the full, raw URL, which should already contain the keyword (perhaps in the domain, perhaps as the name of the webpage).

Twitter itself is a microblogging site, although keywords should be handled somewhat differently, as advised more fully by Ian Gibbins in his guest section on social media marketing. Regarding social media services more generally, Facebook, LinkedIn, MySpace, and Google+ can also all be used in their subtly unique ways to promote your site. Nevertheless, success on any of them depends first and foremost on supplying good content and building a relationship. Search engines are already including real-time content from Twitter and Google+ in their results pages.

Final Word

It's easy to get carried away, but once you know which keywords you're targeting, a simple but important postscriptive warning would be to keep the use of your keywords natural. Don't overdo it and 'over-optimise' your site; use a variety of keywords, and moderately. If you liberally pepper your exact keyword throughout your page(s), you'll deter Google, which is easily smart enough to spot sites that employ 'keyword stuffing', as well as your visitors, who know bad English when they see it. The result: lower rankings, fewer visitors, higher bounce rates and, ultimately, fewer conversions.

Google also employ human evaluators, or 'Quality Raters'. Generally, they don't rate sites individually – their collective results help calibrate Google's search algorithm. Even so, they have been known to flag sites with unusually and unnaturally high frequencies of keywords. And webmasters should know that Google analyses over 200 aspects or 'signals' of your pages (such as its PageRank, its authority, its originality, and its relevance to specific search terms) to determine how much it trusts them. So there is more to internet marketing than *just* keyword research – this is just a reality check to ensure you don't spend so long on keyword research that it's to the detriment of other areas, such as testing your sales letter(s), building a mailing list, adding regular blog posts etc.

Keywords are an incredibly powerful business tool, but their successful application must be tempered by moderation and common sense. Don't use every method of getting your keyword out there – just use those you're comfortable doing yourself, or are happy to outsource to an employee or third party. Taking any kind of action based on your keyword knowledge will, in all likelihood, take you a step ahead of the competition.

Guest Section 1

Search Engine Optimization for Non-Techies

By Ian Greenwood

Search engine optimisation for any website is generally thought of as a good thing! Many webmasters regard it as a crucial aspect to generating traffic, and therefore income, from their website. A huge variety of SEO tactics and strategies are out there, and different experts focus on different techniques that have helped them, or their clients, to be profitable.

There are generally two approaches to optimising any website.

The first is called 'on-page optimisation'. This requires the website developer to execute the optimisation tactics within the HTML code that makes up the site. On-page optimisation includes techniques like manipulating the title tags of each page, and including keywords within meta tags. On-page optimisation can require at least a working knowledge of HTML and website development. As an SEO technique, it's probably way outside the skillset of many business owners and entrepreneurs.

The second approach to SEO is 'off-page optimisation'. This newer approach focuses largely on how your site interacts with other sites and the search engines, rather than on how your HTML technically ticks the boxes of SEO. Off-page optimisation is a more effective approach to SEO than on-page, and has become more popular as the search engines (especially Google) have become more intelligent at ranking content. This SEO strategy also requires little or no knowledge of web coding or HTML, so it's much more within the grasp of site owners, businessmen and women, and entrepreneurs. That's why I concentrate on off-page optimisation in this chapter.

Hi, I'm Ian Greenwood, and about one third of my total traffic for my blog at IanGreenwood.com comes from the search engines. The other two thirds comes from incoming links from high-value/high-traffic sites like Sitepoint.com, but I rarely do any advertising or active marketing for my blog. I currently hold the number two spot on the front page of Google for my keywords (and have done for a number of years now!), and my overall ranking has never been affected by the many 'slaps' handed out by Google over the years.

How do I do it? I call it SEOC, or Search Engine Optimised Content, which I'll outline next.

1. Should I get my web developer to optimise my site?

Most web developers are great at making and building websites, but are sometimes less familiar about how to really optimise their sites for maximum search engine impact. This was obvious when Flash-based sites were all the rage in the early to mid-2000s. These sites were great looking and very animated, graphically intensive and interactive, but were totally impossible for the search engines to spider and rank.

The rule here must be to get the right help to optimise your site – and your web developer is unlikely to be the man (or woman) for the job!

2. Plan your optimisation strategy

The first, and perhaps the most obvious, step is to actually have an optimisation strategy. Developing a website without at least nodding in the direction of SEO is wasted time and effort.

By following the advice laid out in this chapter, you can quickly develop your own strategy for your own site. This of course pays dividends down the road with increased traffic and income (if your site is an ecommerce site, of course).

3. Content is key

One fundamental of SEO planning is that you can do all the SEO you want, but if it's not based on good content then you're wasting your time.

Make sure that the content you're offering on your website is original, valuable and problem solving. The rule is: Always write for the reader, not the search engines! This brings in the best kind of incoming organic links. Other web users link to your content naturally because you have something of value that they want to provide to their readers.

The effect of good-quality content like this is multiplied hugely by also including well-researched keywords within it. This is because the search engines can rank your content and present it easily and accurately within search results. This in turn means that your content is read by those who are most likely to want your information, and want to engage with your web business.

4. Keep your content current

Updating your content increases your rankings within the search results.

By adding fresh, useful content to your website pages on a regular basis, the search engines rate your site as a current site that is updated regularly. This is important to any search engine whose primary focus is obviously serving up relevant, current information. By providing just that, you boost their interest in your site and in your content, and they reward you with a higher page ranking.

5. Type of content

The look and feel of your website is important, but for SEO purposes, it's not as important as the content. Graphic elements within pages, like photos, graphs, pictures or images, all add to the mix of content within the page. This, in turn, boosts the page in the search rankings – especially if the alt tags and the file names of the graphic elements are keyword optimised for the page content.

You can also use other multimedia files as content in this way. Linked audio files, linked video files, database files, PDF documents and email newsletter archives can all be keyword optimised to support your site content and to draw attention from the search engines.

One word of caution here: More does not mean better! Linked multimedia content must be relevant and keyword optimised, otherwise it's just filler. Search engines can't spider an audio podcast or video footage to decide on the content.

Multimedia files need to be identified to the search engine spiders by keywords linked to the file. The obvious way to do this is to name the file with a keyword phrase. For example, an MP3 podcast file may be named something like 'CreatingMarketingStrategies.mp3' instead of 'PodcastMarch2012.mp3'.

So whenever someone searches for 'How do I create marketing strategies', the link to your podcast has a much better chance of making it into the search results. This result would be impossible if the file was called 'PodcastMarch2012.mp3' or something just as nondescript.

By following this simple rule your multimedia files lend weight to your other, easily ranked content, like text.

6. Don't forget internal linking

An easy-to-navigate site helps you in terms of SEO, but many people forget to use internal linking within their site to boost their SEO profile.

When you use linking or anchor text within your site to link to other content, make sure that the linking text is a keyword or keyword phrase, and not just something like 'click here'. By using these keyword anchors, search engines add weight to the link.

You can build up a very user-friendly (as well as SEO-friendly) web of internal links to the content throughout your entire website. Doing so adds weight to the ranking of your site by acting like an inventory of the subjects, themes and topics of the content, as well as helping site visitors to identify individual files and resources.

Another good tip is to always include a sitemap in your website. A *sitemap* is an XML document that essentially lists all the pages and linked files in your site. Search engines like to find these as it makes the job of creating a page inventory much easier.

7. External links – more isn't better

Most people think of link-building in terms of quantity. However, the reality is that the quality of the incoming links is much more important than the quantity.

One simple link from a high-quality site can offer you much better SEO weight than lots of poor-quality links, which can actually hurt your ranking.

Wherever possible, just like your internal links, your external incoming links should be keyword optimised for maximum power. Therefore, try to gain incoming links that say something relevant to the content they link to.

As far as external incoming links go, never underestimate the power of social marketing. Some of the social media and social bookmarking sites are the biggest, and most frequented, sites on the internet. By getting your incoming links from these sites, you can easily boost your site content in the eyes of the search engines.

Always try to get your content linked to from major social bookmarking sites like Digg.com, Delicio.us and Stumbleupon.com. These are three of the major players in the social bookmarking game.

Similarly, links from Facebook.com, Myspace.com, EzineArticles.com, Squidoo.com, Hubpages.com and Youtube.com all lend significant weight to your site. The really great thing about building incoming links through a social media strategy is that in most cases the links are easily within your control. That means you set up the links, and you decide what the anchor text says. (Please, not 'click here'!)

Next steps

I have covered quite a bit in a short amount of space here. So, to sum up, I would advise three paths to better SEO:

1. Broaden your way of communicating. Expand your site content to include video, PowerPoint, podcasts, newsletters, press releases, social content and so forth. The more variety you use when communicating what you have to say, the better you look to the search engines.
2. If you're going to choose just one other form of communication, let it be video. Video is extremely hot right now, and growing in popularity every day. However, video is extremely difficult for the search engines to rank without labelling with keywords. My advice would be to include your video content on a high-traffic video sharing site like Youtube.com and then use their keyword fields and linking facilities to draw in search traffic.
3. Increase your site's search engine ranking by making it easy for your visitors to join in. Add interactive or viral components to your website or blog, such as bookmarking buttons, viral reviews, ratings, visitor comments and sharing tools. This user-generated content has the double benefit of being created by someone else for free and adding greatly to your site's linking and SEO weight.

SEO isn't the black art that some would have you believe. If you create good-quality content for readers, and not search engines, then you're already halfway to a well-optimised site. After that, taking the next few steps isn't that difficult.

Ian Greenwood

www.iangreenwood.co.uk

Guest Section 2

SEO and Site Architecture Case Study

By Walter Mclean

Introduction

This case study shows how the theory in this book can be put into practice in real life situations.

My company Selcom, an IT, web development and hosting consultancy, has developed its own software, *GOWORK*, that allows non-technical people to design and layout websites without requiring any programming or web development skills.

The current website promoting the *GOWORK* product was only a temporary stopgap with very little serious SEO applied. Selcom realised that to be successful it needed to modify its existing website structure to contain keywords that people use when searching online for products that are broadly similar to *GOWORK*.

In this case study I'll show you how I used keyword analysis to find the best keywords, and how these keywords directed both the content and structure of the new website even before designers and copywriters got involved.

Objective

My marketing strategy was to ensure that the *GOWORK* product appears high on page one of Google search within four weeks of the new website going live, to reach as many of the following target audiences as possible:

- **Ecommerce** – small and large companies or individual traders selling products and services online.
- **Company websites** – small and large businesses or single traders who want to control their own online content.
- **Creative design and publishing** – marketing and brand agencies, freelance designers or traditional print-based publishers who want an easy way to publish content online without having to learn any technical web skills.

Ecommerce keywords

Seed word

It is vital that any keywords used throughout the new *GOWORK* website are terms *actually used* by people when searching online. *Ecommerce* was the obvious keyword to use as my starting point, or *seed word*. Using WordTracker as the main keyword strategy tool, I identified that *ecommerce* was the most searched keyword, with an average of 2,234 UK searches per month. This confirmed that I had selected the correct seed word for the ecommerce sector. However, the extremely high competition rate for this term meant that achieving a Google page one rank would be extremely difficult and time consuming.

Related keywords

Further analysis of the data revealed that the combination of the keywords 'ecommerce solutions', 'ecommerce websites', 'ecommerce technology resources' and 'ecommerce UK' totalled 2,205 searches with relatively low competition scores – i.e. high keyword effectiveness index (KEI) figures.

To achieve the objective, I decided to concentrate on these related keywords that potentially provide as many cumulative visitors as 'ecommerce', with substantially less competition and thus a better chance of getting a Google page one position.

Keyword (Phrase Match Format)	Searches	Competition (IAAT)	KEI
"ecommerce"	2,234	35,033,560	0.90
"ecommerce solutions"	1,090	1,467,012	3.18
"ecommerce websites"	563	145,541	17.62
"ecommerce website design"	535	108,515	4.07
"ecommerce software"	527	1,105,614	3.36
"ecommerce website"	518	443,124	1.55
"ecommerce web design"	351	193,918	1.79
"ecommerce hosting"	306	240,650	1.07
"ecommerce technology resources"	280	12	19,600.00
"ecommerce shopping cart"	276	1,433,292	1.54
"ecommerce uk"	272	5,850	9.51
"ecommerce website designers"	255	46,477	17.52
"ecommerce credit card processing"	191	5,378	8.84
"ecommerce company"	186	6,136	7.18
"ecommerce website development"	150	32,785	2.79
"ecommerce technology"	140	5,723	5.73
"ecommerce software solution"	119	15,532	4.38
"content management for websites and ecommerce"	108	1	
"web content management uk"	57	105	27.77

List shows that the term 'ecommerce' has the most monthly searches: Highlighted items show potential average UK monthly search figure of 3,834.

Company website keywords

Questioning your own preconceptions

The keyword analysis for the 'company websites' market sector shows why preconceived ideas of what you may think is the term most people use can actually lead to a trap door and should *always* be challenged.

I initially considered that 'company website' would be the best seed keyword. However, the WordTracker results showed that this term only averaged 305 UK searches per month.

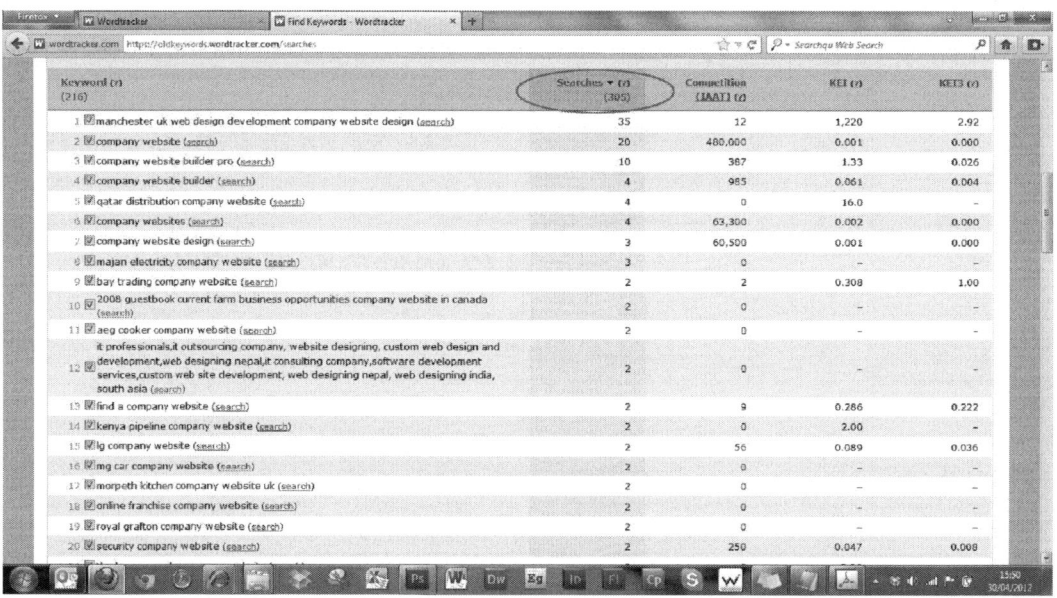

Fig. 22: WordTracker results.

This forced a rethink. By analysing the figures, and through trial and elimination, I discovered that the keyword 'business website' favourably yielded far more results.

Niche keywords

By challenging preconceptions I discovered some niche keywords for this market sector (highlighted below) which people search for. One term in particular, 'business website development', resulted in over four times as many searches as our original seed keyword, 'company website'.

Keyword (Phrase Match Format)	Searches	Competition (IAAT)	KEI
"business website development"	1,334	5,546	416.86
"small business website design"	150	29,609	0.38
"business website packages"	107	571	52.28
"I need a website for my business"	81	796	29.29
"business website builder"	65	9,444	2.29
"corporate website design"	84	14,118	0.17
"web content management system"	123	888,728	1.24
"web based content management system"	61	4,370	4.57
"web content management uk"	57	105	27.77
"web site content management uk"	56	24	174.22
"content management web tool"	48	27	21.53
"web publishing content management system"	48	48	144.00
"web site content management software"	47	1,754	2.99
"online website builder"	184	81,552	1.47
"ecommerce website builder"	81	10,437	3.99
"seo website builder"	77	2,616	2.42

Highlighted items show potential average UK monthly search figure of 1,721.

Creative design keywords

Using your knowledge of the market, product or service

Selcom specialises in delivering IT support and consultancy to the publishing and creative design markets.

Using industry knowledge, analysing competition and knowing the benefits that the *GOWORK* product can deliver, I knew that the keyword 'creative web design' was the most appropriate. There will be occasions when other keywords are more attractive numerically, but if they don't accurately reflect your message then visitors will turn away.

'Creative web design' is a niche term and averages 234 UK searches per month.

Keyword (Phrase Match Format)	Searches	Competition (IAAT)	KEI	KEI3
"creative web design"	234	432,976	2.98	0.00
"creative web design sites"	56	23	522.67	2.44
"website designer software"	75	1,933	9.49	0.04

Selcom was committed to keeping the keyword 'creative web design' because it accurately reflected the *GOWORK* product, but I also needed to increase the amount of searches. Unfortunately, WordTracker and Web CEO did not provide related keywords of any numerical or relevant significance.

Back to basics

Selcom was sure *GOWORK* would appeal to designers and creatives who currently use Adobe Photoshop, InDesign and QuarkXPress applications to design and produce printed material. They may also use these programs to produce visuals for clients to sign-off for website designs.

As *GOWORK* enables designers and creatives to use these skills without having to purchase or learn any other software, a major part of the site will contain small video tutorials on how best to use their Photoshop, InDesign and QuarkXPress skills in tandem with *GOWORK*.

I therefore turned my attention and focus in this direction.

The table below shows that these new keywords not only increased the total number of potential searches but also made the website more relevant for the target audience.

Keyword (Phrase Match Format)	Searches	Competition (IAAT)	KEI	KEI3	Google Count
"creative web design"	234	432,976	2.98	0.00	21,800,000
"creative web design sites"	56	23	522.67	2.44	31,100,000
"website designer software"	75	1,933	9.49	0.04	2,130,000
"InDesign training"	377	13,900	21.21	0.03	436,000
"InDesign course"	201	722	124.69	0.28	265,000
"Photoshop training"	354	112,449	1.58	0.00	5,050,000
"Photoshop course"	193	9,847	5.60	0.02	6,110,000
"quark training"	302	2,374	72.04	0.13	196,000
"quark course"	191	20	1,216.03	9.55	146,000

Highlighted items show potential average UK monthly search figure of 1,918.

Why go to all this bother, even before you have designed your website?

Well, the current temporary website was generating very little traffic and had not generated any substantial sales leads.

The keyword analysis process described in this article provided Selcom with the following benefits:

- Substantially increased potential monthly audience (7,473 searches):
    - Ecommerce – 3,834
    - Business website – 1,721
    - Creative design – 1,918
- Relevant keywords for headings, subheadings and content throughout the new website.

A logical website structure to reflect content and simplify navigation

Content is king

Using the results from the keywords analysis the following structure was created to ensure that the home page and market sector landing pages would contain optimised content for search engines and visitors alike.

Incorporating keywords into the headings and links of the new website helps ensure that navigation is simple and logical for both users and search engines, as shown in the following (simplified) diagram (Fig 23).

Fig. 23. Keywords segmented into three distinct silos.

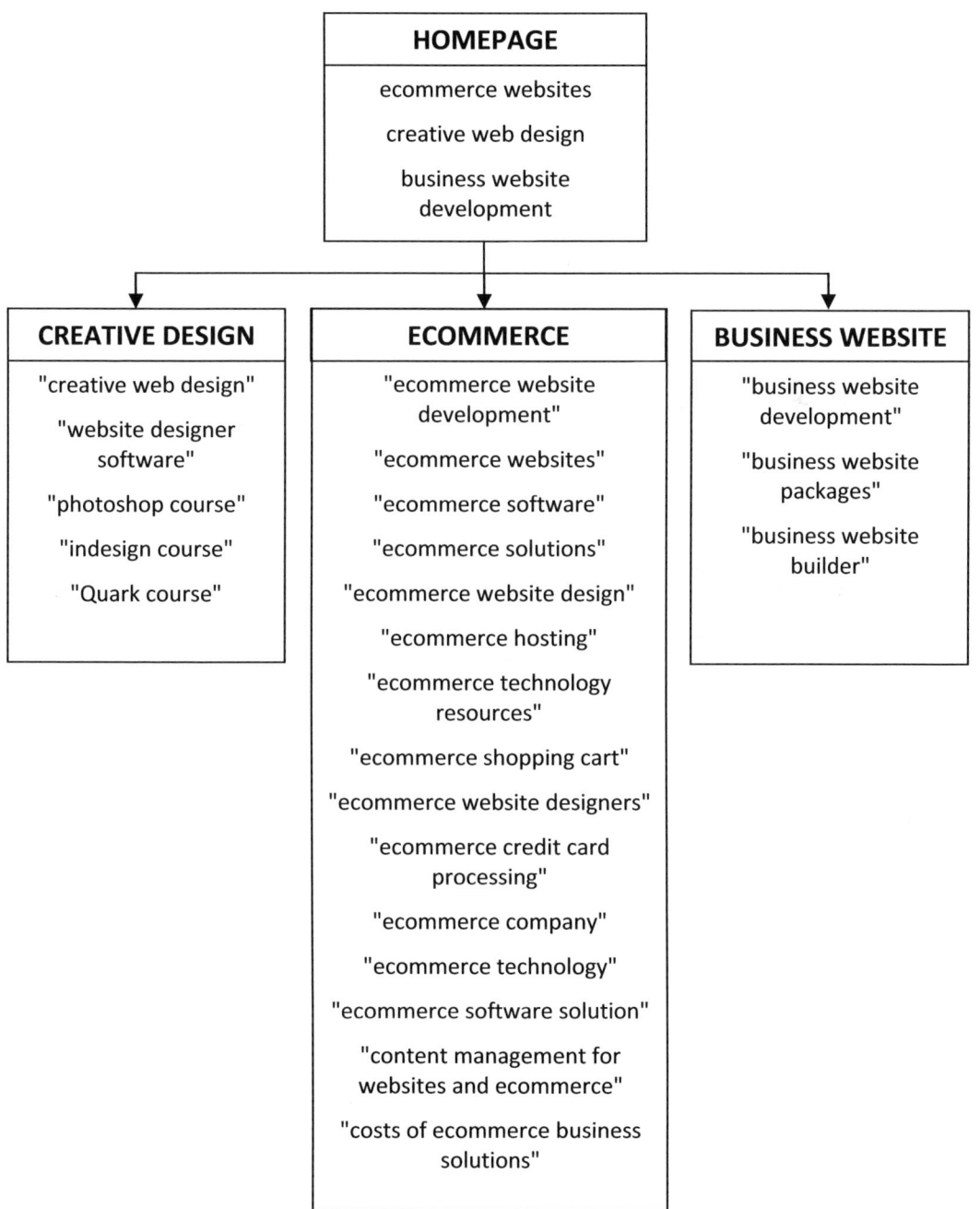

A few keywords are not enough

The keyword process was repeated for the keywords 'headings/links' shown in the above diagram to provide hundreds of other new related keywords, which in turn will be used for other headings, links and page content.

The moral of the story

Perhaps, after reading this article, you will realise that time invested on good keyword analysis is rarely wasted, and that the process will help deliver a website that uses relevant content and a navigation structure that will be attractive to search engines as well as their desired audience.

What's next?

Selcom will now start to design the new website promoting *GOWORK*, for which the structure and content will be based on their keyword analysis findings.

Walter Mclean
Selcom Systems
www.selcom.co.uk
www.gowork.co.uk

Guest Section 3

Applying Keywords To Social Media Marketing

By Ian Gibbins

It's by no means a secret in today's world that consumers are using social networks to find businesses that provide a product or service that they require. They're searching out recommendations for businesses' products and services too, through mutual friends, followers and members of social media groups. Silence is no longer an option with regard to engagement and interaction on social media. If you're a business owner and don't have a presence then you're most certainly losing customers to the competition that's already interacting across the many social media channels available. Now is the time to make your social media presence a priority for your business. Search engines love social media, and also the businesses that are leveraging its power correctly through the use of keywords. However, this is something that shouldn't be rushed into or taken lightly. Take your time to consider the correct use of keywords with your social media, and research the popular keywords related to your business in detail to achieve the best results. Listed below are a number of tips that I'm sure, if followed, will assist you immensely.

1. Incredibly important, but repeatedly overlooked by many businesses when promoting themselves on social media: remembering to include keywords in your profile headline. Although a basic tip, it's highly effective for better search engine optimisation, so think carefully about your choice of keywords. Search engines will certainly pay attention to a highly-targeted, keyword-rich profile headline. The main social media channels, such as Facebook, Twitter and

LinkedIn, are trusted domains so tend to rank higher in the search engine results than your company website with the same keywords. Remember that with Twitter, the 'bio' section serves as the Meta description for the search engines, so you only have 160 characters. Choose your words carefully, and choose the ones that reflect your business the most.

2. Consider the correct use of keywords in the 'about' and 'description' sections of your profile. Although the 'about' sections for Facebook and Google+ are generally made up of one or two sentences, use them as an opportunity to incorporate valuable keywords around your business. When it comes to optimising the 'description' section of your profile then you can really go to town and use the keywords a little more freely. However, still keep the flow of the text natural and be careful not to overuse them. This method can also be applied to the summary section of LinkedIn, which has good search engine authority, but obviously this method isn't so suited to Twitter.

3. As I mentioned earlier, take your time and research your keywords carefully using the Google Keyword Tool. Make a list of all the keywords associated with your business and evaluate them one by one. When considering status updates on Facebook and LinkedIn, tweeting or developing a blog post, take the list of targeted keywords you have chosen and construct a tweet or status update around it. Again, this is a really simple, but highly effective, method of interaction.

4. Andy mentioned earlier about the importance of using social media to share knowledge and valuable information with others, to enable you to build relationships with potential customers and enhance relationships with current ones. Social media allows us to create awareness around our products and services like never before. By creating this awareness around our businesses, people then come to know, like and trust us. I am a great believer in the fact that 'people buy from people', and throughout history this has always been a common thread. The fact is that nothing has really changed, it's just that social media provides us with the tools to make this so much easier. Twitter is without doubt the best tool for creating awareness around our businesses and I would urge you to utilise its power for connecting to huge numbers of followers. However, it's not suited to nurturing a relationship, so I suggest

directing the visitor to another channel where this can take place more easily, such as Facebook or LinkedIn.

5. The use of keywords on Twitter can be made even more powerful through the use of 'hashtags', and I would certainly consider using them. The # symbol is used to mark keywords or topics in a tweet and categorise messages. By using the hashtag before any relevant keywords in your tweets, it will enable your tweets to show up more easily in a Twitter search. For example, from a business promotion point of view when running a recent social media workshop in Portsmouth, I used the hashtag #socialmediaportsmouth, which enabled this to be a link for all search results with tweets containing #socialmediaportsmouth. Whilst this is a very effective method of creating awareness and for promotion, be careful not to overdo it and be seen as spamming. I would suggest use no more than two hashtags in any one tweet, and only use hashtags on tweets that are relevant to your business. That said this will prove to be a really effective way of making your keywords stand out from the crowd!

6. When considering keywords to promote your business through social media, ignore YouTube at your peril! It is the world's second largest search engine behind Google and is an extremely powerful tool for interaction and engagement with customers. Google loves sites to have video on them, as do Facebook and LinkedIn, for the simple reason that it keeps visitors on your page for longer, something I'm sure we would all like to achieve. Of course, YouTube have now made it easy to conduct keyword research through their very own keyword research tool. The first thing you'll notice is the distinct similarities between this one and Google's own keyword research tool. The interface is the same as the Google research tool and the results are displayed in a very similar way. The idea behind the YouTube research tool is that when marketing your business videos on YouTube, you can gain an insight into keyword query popularity and frequency. You can then take these suggestions and integrate them into your video keyword optimisation strategy in the title, video description and tags, leading to increased visibility and targeting of your desired audience.

So as we have seen, keyword research for social media can be an extremely powerful tool in our marketing armoury, and when carried out correctly, can be highly effective in distinguishing which keywords our customers are using. It gives us a better idea of how to construct status updates across Facebook and LinkedIn to communicate our message in the best way, and how to effectively describe and tag videos on YouTube to achieve the greatest results.

The reason I believe social media to be so effective in promoting businesses is the fact that relationships occur naturally online over a period of time. Using highly targeted keywords naturally throughout your posts, blogs, articles and videos, will, I'm sure, also lead to improved results, and you will begin to see an increase on the return of your investment.

Ian Gibbins

Ian is the owner of I.G. Media Marketing Ltd, and has been involved in social media marketing since 2009. Ian specialises in mentoring business owners to leverage and harness the power social media has to offer through one-to-one or group training. Ian is a published author, and released his book The New Guide to Social Media Profits *in 2011. He runs social media workshops and seminars around the UK, and has spoken at events on the subject of social media.*

http://www.igmediamarketing.com

Guest Section 4

Public Relations – How to Inspire, Inform and Create

By Jess Suter

Writing a news release (also known as a press release) can be a tough process, especially for those who are not PR professionals. With online news becoming more and more popular, the writer now has to identify how to make a promotional story not only newsworthy and non-promotional, but also rich with keywords to optimise web traffic.

Don't go over the top with your keywords...

SEO (search engine optimisation) is a great channel to utilise to drive traffic to your website. However, you MUST be careful not to overload your press release with too many keywords – the reason being that when you focus too much on keywords, you run the risk of the search engine not understanding what you have written and, most importantly, the reader not understanding.

How to...

Here are a few tips to keep you on the right track:

Use tools

Use a search engine tool like Google AdWords to discover what relevant keywords people are using – you can then incorporate the most popular (IF they make sense) into your news release.

Remember your audience

Keep in mind that you are writing this news story for the interest of your target audience. Identify what they read and then create your release with the audience AND journalist in mind.

Remember: PR is not all about promoting a company or individual; it's about finding a story that is relevant to the journalist and helpful/beneficial to the reader.

Keep it newsworthy

Nobody wants to hear how wonderful your product is… that isn't news. What they would like to hear is how it could relate to them, the wonders it has done so far, or even whether it's the next 'in' product. If you get stuck on your angle, put your brain into 'brand spotting' mode and look through the web, as well as newspapers, and then you'll see exactly how many stories are printed about products/services, but in a newsworthy way.

Stick to the structure

Apply your keywords to your header, sub-header and introductory paragraph. Use the following structure to ensure effectiveness.

Headline – Make it bold and try to stick to just one sentence.

Sub-header – This is an extension of the headline, but only a small taster.

First paragraph – This is the introductory paragraph; it extends from the sub-header but provides more information and forms a full paragraph.

Second paragraph – Go in-depth, and if you can include statistics, do so here. Here you need to really capture the reader.

Third and fourth paragraphs – These can be quotes from the spokesperson, or a sponsor, or a client.

Summary – Write a small two-/three-sentence summary of your company and insert your web link.

Editor's notes – In this section you can write to the editor about your company/product with the more detailed information that you can't include in your release. REMEMBER: Insert your contact details here too!

Maintain the reader's attention

Make sure you make the paragraphs short and informative in order to engage the reader's interest. The average length of a press release is 300–500 words. You could also create links, using keywords as your anchor text, to relevant sections of your website.

Woo your reader

Remember that although you're sending your release to journalists, they write with the reader in mind – so what the reader likes, the journalist likes. When you're writing, think of the reader. How will they relate to and react to the words? What words will they feel familiar with?

Also try to avoid buzzwords; they can be a massive turn-off for both the reader and the journalist.

Always remember that consistency is key

Mastering an effective press release is great, but when promoting your services/yourself remember that to maintain a good media presence you must be two things: consistent and punctual. In other words, don't promote yourself and then hide for two months, and never miss a deadline for *any* media opportunity. In the media industry, everything has to be done yesterday, so holding out on content or an interview just makes the lead go cold – which can be damaging.

Also remember that when promoting yourself (or even if you hire a PR agent to promote you) you must make time for the media. If a journalist wants to interview you the next day at lunchtime, make sure you're available. It's a fast-paced industry, so to influence your people and raise your profile, your readiness must be taken on board.

To keep on track create the following:

- **PR strategy** – Outline your plans for your first PR year and write notes. What would you like to focus on? Search online for different ways to promote your services. Or you can outsource this to a PR consultant for a small amount.
- **Social media strategy** – Identify whom you're targeting, and plan how you'll engage with your audience online. Again, you can outsource this to an online marketer, PR consultant or specialist in social media.
- **PR timeline** – Create an annual timeline (hopefully from the time you put down this book!). Under each month include a monthly focus – maybe you have a book/service/product you'd like to focus your PR on? Jot down notes. A PR timeline is a very effective way to keep on track with your promotion.

You may also find it beneficial to use a project management tool/software. I personally enjoy using www.hitask.com – not only can you keep on top of your PR, but you can manage your workload in general.

Jess Suter

Jess Suter is the director of The Change PR Ltd, an international ethical PR agency dedicated to helping good people and businesses to inspire, inform and create.

www.thechangepr.com, **@TheChangePR, @Jessica_Suter,** www.facebook.com/TheChangePR

Part 2

Article Marketing

7 What is Article Marketing?

Earlier on I discussed the benefits of keyword research in some depth. That information can be taken and applied in various ways, but one of the single most effective for small and medium-sized businesses (SMBs) is via article marketing.

Keyword research has so many direct uses in your business – and article marketing possesses the same level of versatility. In a single exercise, the benefits to you are numerous, and I'll go into these in the next section. The beauty of the entire end-to-end process is that keyword research and article marketing work together very powerfully.

To paraphrase: performing the keyword research is a fundamentally important exercise, but not acting on the information it provides makes it the definition of a wasted opportunity. On the other hand, article marketing without sufficient keyword research beforehand leaves you optimising your site for commercially undesirable words – again, a wasted opportunity. Put the two together, however, and the likelihood is that you've just taken a *major* step ahead of the competition.

So what is article marketing? Well, what it's not is press releases, although it's very much a form of public relations. In short, non-promotional articles are written on a subject of your choice, with the originals posted on your website. Then, rewritten versions of these articles are submitted to article directories. And that's the crux of it.

Why non-promotional? Articles differ from advertisements – editorially, articles must only contain valuable, unique, impartial information. If it reads like a sales letter, it simply won't be published. It will also contain no images, nor any emphasised text, i.e. bold or italicised text. So an article – more accurately, a 'free reprint article' – is just a headline, and roughly 500 words of plain text.

So exactly what is the purpose? It all comes together at the bottom of the article, where it is permitted to include a short promotional piece of copy in a separate area known as the *reference box* (or *bio box*). The maximum length allowed varies, but generally, it is 450 characters. You can also include links back to your site, which you definitely want, and need, to do. And even though the reference box may only represent 10% of the total content of the article, this must be written very carefully, as it is equally important (if not more so) than the article itself: this is what drives traffic where you'd like it to go.

If you feel comfortable writing one to two articles per week, and have the time to spare, then you could save money by writing them yourself. Allow article writing to form part of your weekly job list. On the other hand, you may prefer to outsource the writing to a third party if workloads mean that you can't spare the time. Article writing services vary immensely in quality; some will write a 500-word article for $5, some for $30. On the article quality spectrum, this puts them all the way between readable and absolutely professional. As with most things money can buy, you get what you pay for, although $10/article is a good target and should get you a perfectly serviceable article.

Let's take a look at some of the direct benefits of a consistent article marketing campaign.

8 Benefits of Article Marketing

The advantages of a well-executed article marketing campaign include – but also go beyond – search engine optimisation. All play their part in their endeavours to increase your bottom line.

Link Building

This is one of the key benefits. A major component of how Google analyses and assesses your own site depends on which other sites link to it, and the *quality* of those sites.

In every article lies the resource box. And in the resource box lies the hyperlink that Google sees pointing back to a page on your website. Search engines like to see interactivity, not isolation, which means outbound and, particularly, inbound links. If Google can see that someone has taken the trouble to link to (and effectively recommend) your site, this stands you in good stead, providing of course that the link comes from a site of some relative value. For example, Google doesn't hold links from sites perceived to be 'content farms' in high regard.

You may have heard of Google's Panda update, which was a change to its ranking algorithm first implemented in February 2011, in what was a determined effort to address content farming. This was a process whereby massive volumes of average or poor articles are written with the sole intention of saturating the search engines and driving traffic to the intended sites out of sheer brute force. It is Google's intention to serve up the best possible content for any search query (who would use a search engine that delivered useless results?); therefore, content farming is at odds with this policy, because the content produced is generally amateurish, valueless text, written to artificially satisfy search engines and *not* the end user. Panda was Google taking steps to penalise such companies. The bad news is that article directories were measurably caught up in this update. The good news is that the Panda update has been developed and improved since, and although article directories are still affected, the situation has calmed down considerably. And at the end of the day, the Panda update does most of us a service because it filters out the lesser sites filled with advertisements and duplicated content.

The bottom line is that high quality, relevant, unique content is king. Google is smart enough to know what is and what isn't, and it's a good idea to play by their rules. You may then ask, is article marketing still worth it? Absolutely, it is. Providing high-quality content on a regular basis, perhaps via a WordPress blog, should be at the core of your website. That way you need never fear changes brought about by Google's ever-evolving algorithms.

Direct Traffic

The source of traffic to your site will be increased in two ways: firstly, from the link at the bottom of the articles themselves; secondly, and more importantly, because of your article marketing campaign, you will have improved the position of your own site in the SERPs, ideally to the first page of Google. And targeted traffic is the name of the game.

Build Your Authority

Articles are an excellent way to increase the exposure of your brand or business; consider them quite rightly as one implementation of public relations. By providing freely accessible, valuable information, you're powerfully positioning yourself as the authority in your area or industry.

If a consistent article marketing campaign is run, your articles will increasingly be shown in the results pages. Few enquiries or sales are made with the first search or site visit, but after appearing several times while researching the product or service they require, your credibility and their trust in you as a subject matter expert increases.

Preselling

Selling on the internet can be quite difficult: unlike a high-street store, there's no one to welcome your visitors personally or answer their questions, and without that direct interaction, building a relationship is that much harder. Websites have to work *hard* to secure a conversion. Therefore, if someone visits your site directly from Google, it's not too dissimilar to cold calling – in short, someone you don't know is asking you to open your wallet. So good sites now offer ways to build trust: guarantees, full contact details, customer service (before, during and after the sale), copywriting and graphics to reassure visitors that any transactions are encrypted and secure.

This is another advantage of article marketing. When someone searching for your products or services (or information relating to it) finds one of your articles, reads it and likes it, they may then wish to click on the link at the bottom to your site. So instead of arriving to your site coldly from Google, they arrive from the article, they already like what you have to say and are interested in reading more and engaging with you further. If the link takes them to a relevant, quality page then the relationship and trust is already being built and (to a realistically partial degree) they have begun the process of being presold on your business.

IP Diversity

This area is slightly more contentious: some SEO experts say this makes a difference, others don't. Personally, I think this should be filed under 'nice to have' at minimum.

What this addresses is the diversity of where your inbound links are coming from. To go to extremes for the sake of illustration: if you had a choice between having 1,000 links from a single site, or only 250 links from 250 sites, you'd be considerably better off opting for the latter. You must be wary of companies that claim to put 1,000s of links up for £5 – the quality of the links will be poor. Far better to get 100 high quality links from a number of high quality, high PageRank sources that Google definitely does not consider to be content farms. Quality beats quantity every time here.

Articles can be submitted to many directories, blogs or article publishers. Many of these are geographically distributed far and wide, as well as having respectable PageRanks of their own: many have PRs of 6 or 7. This variety of inbound links is more appealing and natural to Google than many hundred links from the same server. Each server has its own unique IP (internet protocol) address; hence the term 'IP diversity'.

List Building

As outlined previously, if your definition of a conversion for your website is a sign-up to your mailing list, articles do a terrific job of driving targeted visitors to your site *and* warming them up in the process.

Selling someone on their first visit to your website is hard, but you *can* offer an informative, well-formatted, free report ('Top 10 Tips for X..'), as an 'ethical bribe' in exchange for their name and email address. The result: they have a useful resource, and you captured their basic contact information. Fair trade.

Offering a mailing list has many benefits in its own right: it allows steady, personalised contact with your visitors and keeps them aware of your latest articles and blog posts. Occasionally, a harder-sell mail broadcast can be sent to promote your products. The beauty is that you don't even have to sell your own products: an affiliate link to a relevant, quality, third-party product will cost you nothing, and then see what commission you make from it. A large mailing list, say 1,000+ people, will take time to build, but it is widely regarded as the single most valuable asset of your online business. Expensive, three-day seminars are regularly held solely on the subject of list building.

Article marketing enables another channel to bring in traffic that's already partially familiar with you, and if they've taken the trouble to visit your site from the article, opting into your free mailing list isn't a massive next step for them to take.

Reprints

Owners and publishers of ezines (or online newsletters and magazines) are always on the lookout for new, high-quality content. This is why your article is called a 'free reprint article', because these publishers may choose to republish your article in their publication if it's relevant and timely to a subject they're covering. Part of the deal of republishing them is that although they do so for free, they are also obliged to republish the *complete* article, including the resource box at the bottom.

This is one reason why the main body of the article itself is non-promotional – no publisher will republish an article that offers little information and reads like sales copy for someone else's stuff. However, a discrete section at the end comprised of two or three sentences that offers a short description of who you are, your website and maybe a call to action to download a free report is perfectly acceptable and will be included as a matter of course.

Of course, it's a necessity that you actually hold the copyright to the material in the article. Also, double-check the spelling and grammar; otherwise, it certainly won't be republished.

9 Caveats of Article Marketing

This will be a short section to be sure, but it would be negligent if I didn't mention some of the less advantageous realities of the article marketing process. Even then, one of the perceived drawbacks is actually a distinct benefit.

Firstly, you need to ensure that when you create your onsite article, the URL is *never* changed once the offsite articles are made live. If your article is located at www.thisisanexample.com/article, this is to where all your offsite articles link. If you have a web developer who has a habit of reorganising your site, this must be firmly discouraged. For example, if your developer elects to start categorising your articles like this: www.thisisanexample.com/category/article, then all your offsite articles now point to the wrong place. And it will do your credibility no good if your visitors land on a page with an HTTP 404 (i.e. 'Not Found') error message. So once you have decided on your permalink, ensure it lives up to its name and truly remains a permanent link.

Secondly, if you have outsourced work on your website to a developer, you need a good working relationship, full cooperation and good communications with them. You cannot begin to submit your offsite articles without your onsite articles in place and with the correct path, so it's in your own business interests to ensure this is done to a deadline.

Thirdly, don't be misled into thinking that just a couple of articles will be sufficient. In the same way that *regular* blogs are critical to a blog site, an article marketing campaign requires consistency. This proves to both search engines and your prospects that you are serious and trustworthy, and not an unscrupulous opportunist. Article creation and submission needs to be part of your *Business As Usual* processes – time set aside weekly to ensure you reach an effective, recommended minimum, target of four new monthly articles. Simultaneously it is *not* recommended that you submit more than eight per month, otherwise you risk personally burning yourself out and Google catching wind of the enormous, abnormal number of new inbound links. Four articles a month is a perfectly manageable number – if you feel uncomfortable writing them or don't have time to write them yourself, outsource it to a professional writing service such as www.virtualmissfriday.co.uk or www.textbroker.com.

Lastly, this point concerns your own expectation management: realistically, the results will not be instant. It takes time to write and rewrite the articles, and then they have to be submitted. If you use an article distribution service such as www.submityourarticle.com, once the article is submitted and approved, it is then deliberately trickled out over a default 30 days to thousands of blogs, and hundreds of article directories and email publishers. Even then, each individual directory doesn't always approve an article automatically – it can take a further few weeks for the article to drop into circulation, which is actually a good thing, as this looks all the more natural to Google's ranking algorithms. Finally, Google still has to index all the new offsite articles and adjust the ranking of your page holding the original onsite article. The bottom line is that article marketing isn't an overnight venture, but a long-term *investment*. The good news is that once the work is done and the offsite articles are live, they continue working for you for years to come.

Let's now look at the specifics and practicalities of article marketing in the next section.

10 The Process of Article Marketing

Article Structure

There are three core components of any article: the headline, the body and the resource box:

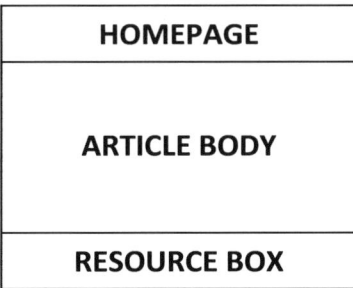

Remember that articles are plain text only: no images or text formatting are permitted. Underline, italics or bold will be stripped when submitted to article directories.

Headline

There are two important things to bear in mind with a headline:

1. You need to include you keyword here. Ideal keywords tend be ones that start with 'how to', as you're directly addressing a problem that people are searching how to resolve.
2. Ensure whoever reads it is compelled to read the entirety of the article. If they don't read the whole article then they won't reach the resource box at the

bottom, which contains your all-important link and call to action. One way to accomplish this is by asking a question in the headline: 'Are You Making This Mistake When Backing Up Your Documents?'

Body

This represents the bulk of the article, and should be around the 500-word mark. Information in here must be non-promotional, valuable, original, easy to read and free of errors, both linguistic and factual. This is your chance to promote your expert knowledge – don't assume people know what you know; *show* them what you know. As a rule, for maximum accessibility it's best to write in non-technical language.

If there's one thing Google isn't a fan of, it's duplicate content. Ensure the article is written in your own words (or the words of your writer); one way to confirm that it hasn't been accidentally plagiarised from another source is to run it through www.copyscape.com.

There are many article directories to which you can submit articles once complete, such as Article Alley, EzineArticles and GoArticles. There are also article submission services that automate the distribution process to many article directories.

It is in the body of the article I recommend you include the keyword twice: once in the first paragraph, and again towards the bottom of the article. Wherever it is inserted, it must read naturally as part of the sentence. If it reads clumsily, or in a contrived manner, two unpleasant things will happen: the chance of it being published decreases (as in most cases, articles are reviewed to ensure they meet editorial standards and guidelines), as does your credibility by anyone reading any of the articles that made it through.

Lists are a simple and effective template for articles: '7 Ways to Maintain Your Computer', or '9 Ways to Lose Weight Using Kettlebells' (headlines aren't sentences and as such don't require a full stop or period at the end). Ultimately, you want the reader to read the whole article and to be impressed by it enough to read the resource box at the end.

Remember that a consistent marketing campaign is key to your ROI, with four to eight articles written and published per month. In addition, results aren't instant. Nevertheless, build enough content with articles submitted *regularly* at this rate for at least six months and you will have generated a commanding network of backlinks to your site.

Resource Box

At the bottom of every article you submit is a short, promotional piece of copy called a resource box (or bio box). Although it's deceptively short with a maximum length of 450 characters (note: not words), it's of equal importance as the main article body, so don't dismiss this section.

This short, but powerful section has two functions:

1. To drive targeted traffic to your website, using a link to an appropriate page or to the homepage itself. Readers can also be directed to a dedicated squeeze page if your intention is to build your mailing list.
2. For SEO purposes, search engines will see the link from this article back to your site. Submitting the article to several directories should have a noticeable effect on your rankings.

You don't have much space in which to do it, but you should provide the following information, written in the third person:

- **Who** you are – mention your name.
- **Why** someone should listen to you – industry experience? Are you an author? Have you won any awards? Are you a member of an organisation?
- **What** they should do now – visit your site? Download a free report? Obtain further information?
- **How** to do that – usually by clicking on a provided link. It's *essential* that this final component has a clear, strong call to action.

It's also permissible to include two links; say one to a relevant onsite page (www.Example.com/TargetPage), and one to the homepage (www.Example.com). It's good practice to use your chosen long-tail keyword as the anchor text to the former, and to use your root keyword as the anchor text for the latter. Don't include more than two links in the resource box.

Post Onsite Article

Now we have an original and complete article, we need to post it on your site. There are myriad content management systems for running and maintaining a website, but by far one of the most popular is WordPress. A new post can easily be created from WordPress' Dashboard area – your website will have its own control panel area. Ask your web developer or administrator to give you a hand if you're unsure.

There are several points worth bearing in mind:

1. In most website management systems, you're allowed to stipulate the URL at which the article is located. For example, you should manually amend it from something random like: http://www.thisisanexample.com/new-post-123 to www.thisisanexample.com/chosen-keyword, hyphenating the keyword. Keep a note of your article's URL – you will need it for the resource box.
2. The 'Title' field is important. This displays at the top of the browser, and gives Google and potential visitors a punchy caption as to what the page is about. Keep this short, and include the keyword. The article headline is normally ideal.
3. Don't forget to populate the 'Description' field. In 160 characters or less, provide two or three naturally written sentences that describe the page content; try to include the keyword just once.
4. There will probably be a keywords field. Paradoxically, this field is actually the least important due to search engines so heavily marginalising them; however, you have little to lose by including say half a dozen (usually comma-separated) targeted keywords.

As an 'optional extra', you could also use a service such as http://pingomatic.com that fires a quick message to various engines to proactively report that your site has been updated. In many cases, this speeds up the site indexing, because you're not waiting for the search engines to crawl your site the next time they're scheduled to. Note: WordPress has a built-in function that does this *automatically* each time you publish a new post.

Rewrite Your Onsite Article

Recall Google's appetite for and love of original content. Despite posting your brand new article on your site first, you will gain far more traction with backlinks from a different, *rewritten* version of that article when we submit it to article directories (as discussed in the next section). We need an original and unique article on your site, and a rewritten version for the directories, because submitting an unaltered version to them would dilute the power of the original, due to the potential for duplicated content.

Several strategies can be employed to help rewrite your article: use synonyms, and perhaps more importantly, logically reorder words, sentences and paragraphs. Use alternative phrases. Take some time to ensure the rewritten article stands in quite sharp contrast to the original. Use Copyscape's (www.copyscape.com/procompare.php) Premium Compare service to check for the rewritten article's uniqueness; aim for it to be at least 70% unique.

There are at least two ways to make life easier when rewriting articles: having software do some of the work, or outsourcing it to an article writing service who do all of the work.

For the former, Spin Rewriter (www.spinrewriter.com) is adept at scanning through an article, understanding the context of each word, and suggesting alternatives that you then choose and select.

Submit Rewritten Article to Directories

Now we have a rewritten article, complete with a resource box, that must be submitted to several article directories, of which there are many.[18] To begin with, start with these three:

- Article Alley: http://www.articlealley.com
- EzineArticles: http://ezinearticles.com
- GoArticles: http://goarticles.com

Create an account with each one, all of which will require you to verify your email. Complete your details in the respective admin areas of each directory – and where applicable, upload a photo of yourself. People buy from people.

You may wish to use a pen name if you cover many niches, for which you will need to create a new email account, perhaps with Gmail. Even if you aren't involved with niche publishing, it's still not a bad idea to create a new email account, since you will tend to receive a considerable number of update and notification emails as your articles are submitted, approved and published. This organises all your article-related emails into a separate silo.

If the article is rejected, the editorial team normally explain clearly why. Sometimes the article may not be long enough; sometimes they may feel a keyword has been overused. It is then simply a case of correcting the problem and resubmitting it.

It's worth noting that some directories allow full HTML resource boxes and others use plain text boxes. The content of your resource box does not need to change, apart from an amendment to the link. For example, with an **HTML resource box**, anchor text can be used to link to the onsite article:

> *"To read more about da Vinci's paintings and download a free report, visit our site at www.ExampleDaVinciSite.com now."*

---

[18] A comprehensive list can be found here: http://www.vretoolbar.com/articles/directories.php.

In this instance, 'da Vinci's paintings' is actually a link to a highly relevant page such as www.ExampleDaVinciSite.com/da-vinci-paintings/da-vinci-portrait. And just for good measure, the site's home page is included in plain text at the end.

With a **plain text resource box**, only the link is allowed and keywords cannot be applied to anchor text. Therefore, the same text would have to become adapted to the following:

> *"To read more about da Vinci's paintings and download a free report, visit our site at www.ExampleDaVinciSite.com/da-vinci-paintings/da-vinci-portrait now."*

Note: we have lost the first link, and the second link is longer. However, because we included the keyword in the onsite article's URL, the link *and* keyword are still both working for us.

Remember that the directories listed above should be used to familiarise yourself with the process. Once you have gained confidence, articles should be submitted to more directories. The more directories you submit to, the more you reap the advantages that article marketing offers, including backlinks, improved search engine rankings and, ultimately, conversions. So when you are ready, create accounts and submit your articles to this next set of directories:

- ArticlesBase: http://www.articlesbase.com
- Buzzle: http://www.buzzle.com
- IdeaMarketers: http://www.ideamarketers.com
- WryteStuff: http://wrytestuff.com

Automating Submissions

There is an alternative to submitting articles to directories manually. Once the original article is rewritten, it could then be submitted to a paid article distribution service *once*, which then does all of the work of farming it out to dozens of directories. Submit

Your Article (www.submityourarticle.com) is one such service, and I have used it professionally for years.

Once the account is set up – which does involve creating accounts with half a dozen or so article directories – articles can then be entered in a largely fire-and-forget manner. Automating the process has several distinct advantages:

1. *Efficient use of time*. Submitting articles manually can be time-consuming. Automating it increases your productivity in the same period substantially, as the article only needs to be entered once.
2. *Better coverage*. The more article directories you submit to, the merrier. Submit Your Article currently posts articles to a network of roughly 300 article directories, 2,000 blogs and around 650 email publishers. Try doing *that* manually!
3. *Editorial review*. Your articles must be high quality, and meet standards laid down by the various directories. This step offers another layer of double-checking before your article goes public.
4. *More natural distribution*. The chances are that if you submit several articles manually, they will all be done the same day, while it is the active task; it is far better to submit them more gradually over a period of weeks. Automating the submissions allows them to be 'trickled out' in a controlled, hands free, regular manner that looks far more natural to the search engines. Typically, an article is distributed over the course of 30 days.
5. *'Naked' articles*. Another powerful application of some automated services is that articles are not only submitted to directories, but also to blogs, of which there are considerably more. These are called naked articles because they are published *without* the resource box. So what's the point in using them, if all links and promotional copy are stripped from the article? Instead of residing in the resource box, one or two links are now included cleverly in the *main body* of the article. Plain text links are not allowed – HTML links must be used, whereby the anchor text must form a natural part of the sentence. In other words, *with or without the link*, the text must read fluidly and normally. And it is absolutely worth taking a little extra effort to do.

Spintax

There is a final, major advantage to using a submission service.

Up until now, we have submitted identical copies of the same rewritten article to all the directories. It turns out there is quite a straightforward way of automating the distribution of unique variations of this article to each and every directory. This way, the search engines begin to perceive a 'cloud' of *unique* articles linking to your site, which in all likelihood will boost your rankings even further.

Instead of the usual plain text we would write normally, we introduce an article-specific syntax known as *spintax* (a portmanteau word that combines 'spin' and 'syntax'), which you could think of as a *very* simple programming language.

Spintax uses curly brackets to group alternative words, and the vertical bar (or 'pipe') to separate them. By way of an example, in our article we could have originally written:

> *The cat sat on the mat.*

And every article would contain this single sentence. However, with spintax, we could rewrite it as:

> *The {cat|dog} {sat|crouched|played} on the {mat|floor}.*

If this was included and correctly entered into a distribution service, then one of *twelve* variations would be randomly submitted to the different directories, as different words (separated by the pipes) are chosen:

Directory A: *The cat sat on the mat.*

Directory B: *The cat sat on the floor.*

Directory C: *The cat crouched on the mat.*

Directory D: *The cat crouched on the floor.*

Directory E: *The cat played on the mat.*

Directory F: *The cat played on the floor.*

Directory G: *The dog sat on the mat.*

Directory H: *The dog sat on the floor.*

Directory I: *The dog crouched on the mat.*

Directory J: *The dog crouched on the floor.*

Directory K: *The dog played on the mat.*

Directory L: *The dog played on the floor.*

Now extrapolate that to an article with *dozens* of sentences rewritten in this manner: it's perfectly possible to create thousands of unique articles using this system, if you ever could submit that many.

Lastly, spintax allows 'nesting', whereby alternative words or phrases can be layered *within* other alternative words or phrases, compounding the number of possible variations. For example, consider the following sentence:

> The {cat|dog} {sat|crouched|played} {on the {mat|floor}|in the {garden|conservatory}}.

This example alone would generate 24 unique variations. Spintax has the potential to add significant firepower to your article marketing campaigns. However, extreme care must be taken to ensure every possible resulting sentence reads naturally; otherwise, they may not meet the usually quite tough editorial standards. It can take a little time to fine-tune sentences written in this way to get them working and reading 'just right'.

With a little practice, entire articles can be rewritten in this way. If this sounds daunting, they can be written professionally using a service such as Virtual Miss Friday (www.virtualmissfriday.co.uk), who refer to these as *Advanced ArticleLeverage* articles.

Private Label Rights

You may have come across Private Label Rights (PLR) articles. These articles are generally nonexclusively licensed (so you won't be the only person using them), low quality and widely circulated, none of which are beneficial to your business.

Always remember that great content and value to users must come first. PLR articles are a good way to generate *ideas* for articles, but you'd be wise not to publish them directly without first rewriting them to within an inch of their life. And with the time you spent making the necessary extensive changes, it may be quicker to write an original article from scratch anyway.

The worst-case scenario is *not* that inferior, mass replicated articles will just have zero effect on your site rankings, but that your site will actually be actively harmed and measurably penalised.

Summary

Here's a concise review of the article marketing process:

1. Identify your long-tail keyword(s).
2. Write an article relevant to that keyword. Alternatively, have it written by a third party.
3. Post the article (but not the resource box) on your own site.
4. Rewrite the article, or have it rewritten, and check its uniqueness with www.copyscape.com. In addition, write an effective resource box, or have one written. It's critical that the resource box has a link to the onsite article.
5. Manually submit them to article directories, or automate the process with an article distribution service.
6. Repeat the process, submitting four to eight articles per month.

Practice makes perfect: as the process becomes more familiar, it becomes easier. Article marketing has grown significantly in its number of users and the strength of its application in the last five years. Combined with a small, but well-researched, batch of keywords, few processes are likely to give you a greater return for your business.

Guest Section 5

Copywriting Tips for Articles

By Frank Edwards

How to write great article titles

If you intend to use article marketing to sell your products, gain credibility and brand yourself as an authority in your niche then writing informative articles is a great way to achieve these things.

But the content of your article is only half the story. One of the most challenging parts of your article is getting someone to read it in the first place. And two of the most critical elements you need to consider in every article you write are the headline and keywords.

In the world of mass media, including newspapers, magazines and advertising, the importance of the headline is well known. In fact, one of the greatest advertising men of all time, David Ogilvy, stated that 80% of your time should be spent crafting and writing your headline so that your material stands out from the crowd and makes the reader interested in the content.

Think about it... You could have an article packed with the best information that will help your readers, but it's no good if the headline of your article doesn't grab their attention – or even worse – they can't find it in the first place.

There are many different formulas for crafting headlines. These formulas are used day in, day out in the media industry and some of the best headlines have two things in common: *curiosity* and *self-interest*. Curiosity is used to stop the reader in their tracks and self-interest is used to lure them into the body copy, as it hints there might be something of great benefit to them personally if they read more of the article.

The trick with online content and articles is to incorporate your keywords into your titles so they get found easily, communicate what the gist of your article is about and provoke curiosity and self-interest in the reader. One of the easiest ways to incorporate keywords in your title is to place them at the beginning. Here are some examples if your article is about dachshund dogs...

> *"Dachshunds: 5 Top Tips to Keep Your Dachshund Fit and Healthy"*

> *"Dachshund Training: Are You Making These Mistakes When Training Your Dachshund?"*

Or even more keyword targeted...

> *"Miniature Smooth-Haired Dachshunds: 3 Things You Must Avoid Feeding Your Dachshund to Prevent Expensive Vet Bills"*

As you can see, these titles incorporate the elements of curiosity, self-interest and appropriate keywords.

Use this technique whenever you write sales letters, emails, articles or ebooks, and your content will be read more often.

The Resource Box – how to make it memorable

The resource box at the end of your article is your opportunity to drive traffic to your website – or anywhere else – so use it wisely. It's your last chance to tell people who you are and what you do.

However, you must write your resource box in such a way that it offers the reader a BENEFIT of going to the destination of your choice.

Always remember that benefits sell. The resource box is your opportunity to sell the reader further services, goods and products that you're using your articles to drive them towards.

So don't say something like, *"My name is Joe Bloggs and here is my website."* That's dull and uninspiring. Readers need specific instructions and a reason to go where you want them to.

Therefore, a better resource box would look something like this:

"Joe Bloggs is a dachshund breeder and trainer who publishes 'Dachshund World' – a weekly dachshund Newsletter. Subscribe free at www.[domain name].com."

An even better resource box will include backlinks to your website domain, or to your original article on the site.

To get quality traffic to your site it's important to have back-links to the pages you're promoting and to improve your search engine rankings.

So an even better resource box would look something like this:

"Joe Bloggs is a dachshund breeder and trainer who publishes 'Dachshund World' – a weekly dachshund Newsletter, containing many popular reports and articles by world renowned dachshund experts.

For more information like this and to download the latest free newsletter go to his dachshund website and subscribe free at www.[domain name].com."

Remember, the internet changes very rapidly and what works today may not work tomorrow. So always check with your article directory or submission service for their current rules regarding the contents of resource boxes.

Frank Edwards
Copywriting and Direct Response Marketing
www.frank-edwards.com

Appendix

Keyword tools

Free

Google AdWords Keyword Tool:
https://adwords.google.com/select/KeywordToolExternal

Google Insights for Search: http://www.google.com/insights/search

Soovle: http://soovle.com

Lexical FreeNet: http://www.lexfn.com

Wordtracker: https://freekeywords.wordtracker.com

SEOmoz: http://www.seomoz.org/keyword-difficulty

WordStream: http://www.wordstream.com/keywords

Trellian Keyword Discovery: http://www.keyworddiscovery.com/search.html

SEO Book Keyword Suggestion Tool: http://tools.seobook.com/keyword-tools/seobook

Honourable Mention: Google Wonder Wheel (now officially offline, probably permanently).

Paid

Niche Profit Classroom (Keyword Advantage tool) ($67/month):
http://www.nicheprofitclassroom.com

Wordtracker ($69/month): http://www.wordtracker.com

Compete (Pro services from $199/month):
https://www.compete.com/plans/#detailed_comparison

SEOmoz (from $99/month): http://www.seomoz.org/plans

WordStream (from $329/year): http://www.wordstream.com/seo-pricing

SpyFu (from $79/month): http://www.spyfu.com

KeywordSpy (from $89.95/month): http://www.keywordspy.com

Article writing and rewriting services

Virtual Miss Friday: http://www.virtualmissfriday.co.uk/submityourarticle

Textbroker: http://www.textbroker.com

Article spinning services

Spin Rewriter: http://www.spinrewriter.com

SpinChimp: http://spinchimp.com/

Article distribution services

Submit Your Article: http://www.submityourarticle.com

Content Crooner: http://www.contentcrooner.com

Article directories

Article Alley: http://www.articlealley.com

EzineArticles: http://ezinearticles.com

GoArticles: http://goarticles.com

Internet marketing communities

Internet Marketing Review (Paid): http://www.internetmarketingreview.com

The Warrior Forum (Free): http://www.warriorforum.com

PPC services

AdWords Answers: http://www.adwordsanswers.com

Perry Marshall's Definitive Guide to Google AdWords:
http://www.perrymarshall.com/adwords

Web browsers

Chrome: https://www.google.com/chrome

Firefox: http://www.mozilla.org/en-US/firefox

Miscellaneous

GoDaddy (Domain registration service): http://www.godaddy.com

AWeber (email opt-in and marketing service): http://www.aweber.com

WordPress (a free and popular blogging tool): http://wordpress.org

ClickBrief (Internet marketing newsletter): http://www.smartbrief.com/news/clickbrief

Keyword research services

Andrew D. Mason Keyword Research: http://www.keywordresearchservice.co.uk

WebSearch SEO: http://www.websearchengineranking.com/keyword-research

www.iProspect: http://www.iprospect.co.uk

Glossary

Affiliate marketing – Affiliates earn a commission from selling a merchant's products that the affiliate promotes themselves.

Anchor text – The wording of a hyperlink. 'Click here to read more' and 'Download your free report on how to improve your golf swing' contain underlined examples.

Bounce rate – The percentage of visitors who leave within moments of landing on your site. This should be kept under 50-60%.

CMS – Content management system; a platform for running and maintaining a website. A popular example is WordPress.

CPA – Cost per action. A commission is paid if a desired action is taken, not necessarily a sale. For example, if your site triggers someone to sign up to a mailing list, you will still be paid a commission.

CPV – Cost per conversion. The cost of acquiring a customer, calculated from the cost of the campaign divided by the number of direct conversions received.

CTR – Clickthrough rate. The number of times a link is actually clicked divided by the number of times it's displayed, expressed as a percentage.

CVR – Conversion rate. The number of conversions (sales or enquiries) divided by the number of website visits. Sales copy is one of many important factors that can affect the conversion rate.

Impressions – The number of times an advert is displayed onscreen.

Offsite article – The rewritten article that is replicated many times with the use of article directories and other channels.

Onsite article – The single, original, unique article that sits on your website.

PageRank – A value between 0-10 that Google assigns every webpage, based on Google's estimation of its importance, influence, authority and trustworthiness.

PPC – Pay per click, a method of paying search engines to direct targeted traffic to your site.

SEM – Search engine marketing. An umbrella term that covers both SEO and PPC.

SEO – Search engine optimisation. Methods and processes for improving the visibility and relevance of your site within the various search engines.

SERPs – Search engine results pages. These are the pages seen immediately after searching for a term; you probably want your site(s) to show on the first page.

SMB - Small and medium-sized businesses.

Squeeze page – A landing page with an opt-in form and no outbound links, created primarily for list-building purposes.

Bibliography

Ron Jones, *Keyword Intelligence: Keyword Research for Search, Social, and Beyond*, John Wiley & Sons, 2011.

Colette Mason, *Social Media Success in 7 Days*, lulu.com, 2011.

Chris Anderson, *The Longer Long Tail: How Endless Choice is Creating Unlimited Demand*, Random House Business, 2009.